CAMPAIGN 421

SINAI 1916–17

The Fight for the Suez Canal

STUART HADAWAY ILLUSTRATED BY GRAHAM TURNER

OSPREY PUBLISHING
Bloomsbury Publishing Plc
Kemp House, Chawley Park, Cumnor Hill, Oxford OX2 9PH, UK
Bloomsbury Publishing Ireland Limited,
29 Earlsfort Terrace, Dublin 2, D02 AY28, Ireland
1385 Broadway, 5th Floor, New York, NY 10018, USA
E-mail: info@ospreypublishing.com
www.ospreypublishing.com

OSPREY is a trademark of Osprey Publishing Ltd

First published in Great Britain in 2025

© Osprey Publishing Ltd, 2025

All rights reserved. No part of this publication may be: i) reproduced or transmitted in any form, electronic or mechanical, including photocopying, recording or by means of any information storage or retrieval system without prior permission in writing from the publishers; or ii) used or reproduced in any way for the training, development or operation of artificial intelligence (AI) technologies, including generative AI technologies. The rights holders expressly reserve this publication from the text and data mining exception as per Article 4(3) of the Digital Single Market Directive (EU) 2019/790

A catalogue record for this book is available from the British Library.

ISBN: PB 9781472867797; eBook 9781472867803; ePDF 9781472867810; XML 9781472867780

25 26 27 28 29   10 9 8 7 6 5 4 3 2 1

Maps by Bounford.com
3D BEVs by Paul Kime
Index by Richard Munro
Typeset by Lumina Datamatics Ltd
Printed by Repro India Ltd

Osprey Publishing supports the Woodland Trust, the UK's leading woodland conservation charity.

To find out more about our authors and books visit www.ospreypublishing.com. Here you will find extracts, author interviews, details of forthcoming events and the option to sign up for our newsletter.

For product safety related questions contact productsafety@bloomsbury.com

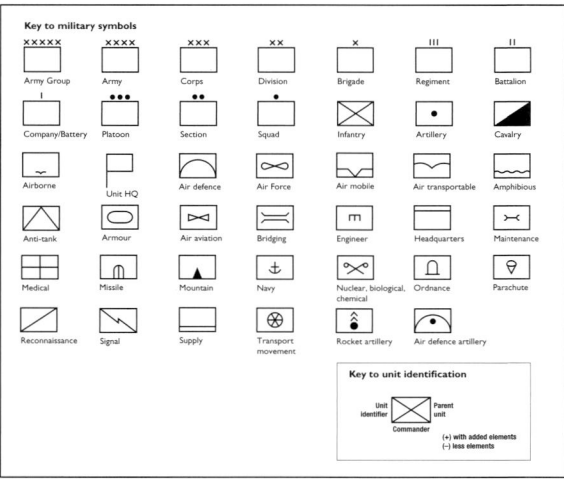

Acknowledgements

The author would like to thank the following individuals for their assistance: Bill Anderson, Lee Barton, Brianne Bellio and Alex Boulton at Osprey Publishing, Dr Hamza Bilgü, Mark Bristow, David Buttery, Graham Caldwell, Col. Stamford Cartwright of the Queen's Own Worcestershire Hussars Museum, Edward Dingle of the Light Horse and Field Artillery Museum (Nar Nar Goon, Victoria), Aaron Fox, Nina Hadaway and the staff of the Auckland War Memorial Museum.

Photographs

All photos unless otherwise noted are Author's Collection.

Artist's note

Readers may care to note that the original paintings from which the colour plates in this book were prepared are available for private sale. The Publishers retain all reproduction copyright whatsoever. All enquiries should be addressed to:

Graham Turner, PO Box 568, Aylesbury, Bucks, HP17 8EX, UK
www.studio88.co.uk

The Publishers regret that they cannot enter into any correspondence regarding this matter.

Abbreviations

AFC	Australian Flying Corps
ALH	Australian Light Horse
A&NZ	Australian and New Zealand (Mounted Division)
ANZAC	Australian and New Zealand Army Corps
CTC	Camel Transport Corps
EEF	Egyptian Expeditionary Force
EI&ESS	East Indies and Egypt Seaplane Squadron
ELC	Egyptian Labour Corps
FA	Flieger Abteilung
HAC	Honourable Artillery Company
HK&S	Hong Kong and Singapore
HMS	His Majesty's Ship
ICC	Imperial Camel Corps
MEF	Mediterranean Expeditionary Force
NZMR	New Zealand Mounted Rifles
QF	Quick Firing
QOWH	Queen's Own Worcestershire Hussars (Yeomanry)
RA	Royal Artillery
RE	Royal Engineers
RFA	Royal Field Artillery
RFC	Royal Flying Corps
RGH	Royal Gloucestershire Hussars (Yeomanry)
RHA	Royal Horse Artillery
RNAS	Royal Naval Air Service
RSF	Royal Scots Fusiliers
SMLE	Short Magazine Lee–Enfield

Front cover main illustration: Taking the Reduit at El Magruntein, 9 January 1917. (Graham Turner)
Title page photograph: Ottoman forces defend trenches in the eastern Sinai. (Author's Collection)

CONTENTS

INTRODUCTION	5
CHRONOLOGY	8
OPPOSING COMMANDERS	10
Ottoman . British	
OPPOSING FORCES	17
Ottoman . British . Orders of battle	
OPPOSING PLANS	28
Ottoman . British	
THE CAMPAIGN	32
Building their logistics . Affair at Qatia . Digging in at Romani . Battle of Romani . Pursuit from Romani . Bir el Mazar . Border battles	
AFTERMATH	89
THE BATTLEFIELD TODAY	92
BIBLIOGRAPHY	94
INDEX	95

The Sinai Desert, 1916

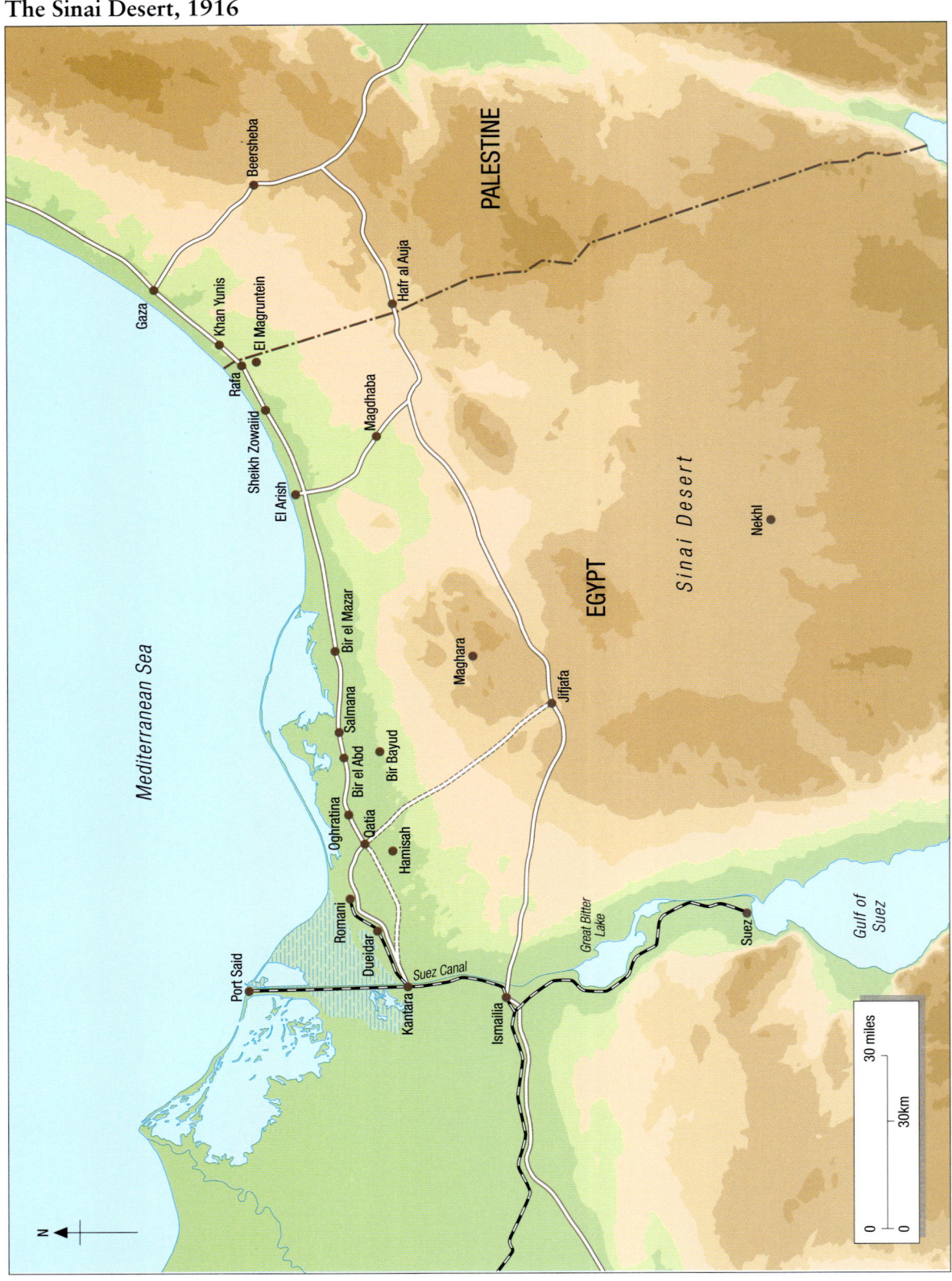

INTRODUCTION

The Suez Canal was, as proclaimed Kaiser Wilhelm II, the 'jugular vein of the British Empire'. Oddly, Britain had shown little interest when it was being built as a largely Franco-Egyptian concern in the 1860s, but after opening in 1869 it became clear what a crucial link in the Imperial network the Canal would be. By 1880, British factories accounted for over a quarter of the world's industry, and by 1913, nearly half the world's merchant shipping was British, ferrying raw resources to its factories and then the finished products out across the globe. The short cut through the Suez Canal, from the Mediterranean to the Red Sea, cut over 6,200km (3,900 miles) off the route from India to Britain. On repeated round trips over the course of a year, this became a significant factor, and without the Canal, nearly half as many merchant ships again would have been needed to maintain the same flow of supplies. This link was under the control of (for the British) dubious foreign interests. Egypt was a part of the Ottoman Empire, although it did have significant autonomy, while Imperial tensions with France were a constant source of concern. When the Egyptian government was forced to default on its loans in 1875, Britain was there to lead the international effort to bail it out. When the Egyptian Army led a revolt against foreign interference in 1882, Britain was left alone by its European partners to suppress the uprising and re-impose outside civil authority. By the time the dust settled, Britain was effectively in control of Egypt, initially through tight supervision of its finances, and increasingly through its legal, military and civil authorities. Although Egypt remained a 'semi-independent vassal state of the Ottoman Empire', as the Foreign Office termed it, and would continue to pay its taxes to the Ottoman Sultan until the outbreak of World War I, Egypt had become a de facto part of the British Empire.

Britain would go to great lengths to protect Egypt, fighting several campaigns in Egypt and the Sudan in the 1880s and 1890s, and coming close to war with the Ottomans in 1906–08 during the 'Taba Crisis'. This was over the exact positioning of the border between Egypt and Greater Syria, the latter being the Ottoman province that bordered the eastern side of the Sinai Desert, and the southern portion of which was commonly known as Palestine. At the outbreak of World War I, Britain's dependence on the Canal became even more evident. With the needs of an industrialized world war to feed, the raw resources from India, South East Asia, the Pacific, Australia and New Zealand were all needed more than ever. Rubber, tin, fresh and frozen meat, wheat, timber, horses and that most indispensable of war materials, tea, were all needed to feed Britain's troops and factories.

The Suez Canal was a critical cog in feeding Britain's industry in peacetime. In wartime, critical supplies flowed through it on their shortest routes to British, French and Italian factories.

And many of those troops were also coming up the Canal. Between August and December 1914, some 164,000 troops moved north through the Suez Canal as Britain withdrew its Imperial garrisons and called on the Indian Army to bolster the battered British Expeditionary Force in Belgium and France, and hold the line until Kitchener's Volunteers could be trained.

Among those men were the first 20,000 Australian and New Zealand volunteers. Few had more than a few weeks of training, and they were offloaded into the desert around Cairo to be turned into effective military units. From the other direction came the 42nd (East Lancashire) Division of the Territorial Forces, sent to complete their training and form a garrison for Egypt. Neither contingent was capable of effective war operations, and so to protect the Suez Canal, two further actions were taken. The Sinai Desert was abandoned; it was too large and open, and any garrison forces would be too easily isolated and overwhelmed. Instead, a line was established largely behind the Canal, with just a few outposts on the eastern bank. Secondly, several Indian Army brigades (later increased to two divisions) were temporarily retained in Egypt to guard the Canal.

The Ottoman Empire had signed a treaty with Germany, with which it had strong military and commercial ties, in August 1914, and at the end of October that year, it reluctantly entered the war as one of the Central Powers. In January 1915, an expeditionary force under the command of Ahmed Djemal Pasha, the Ottoman Governor of Syria and commander of the 4th Army, with much of the actual staff work being undertaken by his German Chief of Staff, Colonel Friedrich Freiherr Kress von Kressenstein, crossed the Sinai Desert and attacked the Suez Canal. Their attack was relatively easily defeated by the Indian Army garrison during the first week in February, and Djemal Pasha withdrew. No British forces were available to mount a pursuit and Kressenstein was left behind with a small force of regular and irregular troops to maintain a harassing pressure on the Canal. Any plans for a second attack in 1915 were forestalled by the British, Indian, French, Australian and New Zealand landings in the Dardanelles in April 1915. This force, the Mediterranean Expeditionary Force (MEF), was based in Egypt, and all of the troops and resources in that country were concentrated on supporting the landings, while the Ottomans were forced to also refocus their efforts in that direction.

The war in the Sinai Desert largely lay fallow for the rest of 1915, and in the early days of 1916, the MEF was withdrawn to Egypt. Now under the command of Sir Archibald Murray, most of its units were earmarked for redeployment to the Western Front (although one division was despatched to Mesopotamia). However, four infantry divisions and several independent cavalry brigades were retained in Egypt under the command of Murray. On 10 March 1916, these forces were designated as the Egyptian Expeditionary Force (EEF), given the task of advancing into the Sinai Desert and establishing a forward line of defence for the Suez Canal. Within a week, the Australian Light Horse and New Zealand Mounted Rifles brigades would be brought together to form the Australian and New Zealand (A&NZ) Mounted Division, although the exact composition of the division varied over time.

The British garrison in Egypt (like these men of the Suffolk Yeomanry) had been on the defensive during 1915 or supporting the Gallipoli campaign. (Colourized by Tom Marshall)

Members of the Norfolk Yeomanry on a rifle range in the Sinai, Christmas 1916.

CHRONOLOGY

1914

1 August	Germany and the Ottoman Empire sign a secret treaty.
4 August	Britain declares war on Germany.
8 September	Indian troops start arriving in Egypt.
27 September	42nd (East Lancashire) Division begins arriving in Egypt.
29 October	The Ottoman Empire attacks Russia.
2 November	Martial Law declared in Egypt.
3 November	Royal Navy warships bombard Ottoman forts on the Dardanelles.
5 November	Britain declares war on the Ottoman Empire.
17 November	The first detachment of the Royal Flying Corps arrives in Egypt.
3 December	The first convoy of ANZAC troops arrives in Egypt.
18 December	Egypt declared a British Protectorate.

1915

3 February	First Battle of the Suez Canal.
25 April	British landings in the Dardanelles mark the start of the Gallipoli campaign.
20 December	British and ANZAC troops withdrawn from Suvla Bay and Anzac Cove on the Gallipoli Peninsula.

1916

8 January	British forces withdrawn from Cape Helles, marking the end of the Gallipoli campaign.
February	Work begins on a railway into the Sinai Desert, to supply British forces once the advance begins. A pipeline soon follows, although work on this is slower.
10 March	Lieutenant-General Sir Archibald Murray placed in command of all forces in Egypt. These are now to be known as the Egyptian Expeditionary Force (EEF).
23 April	Ottoman tactical victory but strategic failure at Qatia and Oghratina.
5 June	Opening shots of the Arab Revolt.
9 July	Arab forces capture Mecca.

3–5 August	EEF victory in the Battle of Romani.
12 August	EEF pursuit called off.
15–17 September	Raid on Bir el Mazar.
4 December	Ottoman high command decide to withdraw completely from the Sinai.
21 December	EEF occupies El Arish.
23 December	EEF captures Ottoman garrison at Magdhaba.

1917

9 January	EEF captures Ottoman garrison at El Magruntein (Rafa).

British Yeomen sit in an improvised bivouac in the Sinai.

OPPOSING COMMANDERS

OTTOMAN

Djemal Pasha was in a similar position to Murray, with civil and military responsibilities running far outside just the Sinai. (Public domain, via Wikimedia Commons)

Ahmed Djemal (or Cemal) Pasha was born in Greece in 1872. He joined the Ottoman Army in 1890 and graduated from the Ottoman Staff College in 1893. He became a member of the Committee of Union and Progress (CUP), one of the various bodies collectively known as 'Young Turks' who were pressing for reform in the Ottoman Empire. He served in Salonika, and became the Military Inspector of Railways. He was in Constantinople during the 1908 revolution that saw the CUP force the dictatorial Sultan to reintroduce the Constitution and recall the parliament. He also took part in suppressing the resulting 1909 counter-revolution, which ended with the replacement of the Sultan with his more liberal half-brother. The civil unrest caused by these changes included a series of massacres against Armenians in the Adana region, and Djemal was despatched to restore order, hanging many of the perpetrators and supporting the Armenian population. In 1911, he briefly became the Military Governor of Baghdad before returning to the field army to fight in the First Balkan War (1912). In January 1913, he played a leading role in the CUP coup that led to its seizure of power in the Ottoman Empire, and he was appointed Military Governor of Constantinople. By the end of the year, he had received the title 'Pasha'. In early 1914, he was appointed Minister of the Ottoman Navy, forming a triumvirate to rule the Empire with Enver Pasha (War Minister) and Talaat Pasha (Interior Minister).

On the outbreak of war in 1914, Djemal was despatched to become Military Governor of Greater Syria, a role that encompassed all military, political and administrative matters across Syria, Palestine, the Trans-Jordan,

Mesopotamia, Arabia and (nominally) Egypt. This included taking command of the 4th Army, and he immediately threw himself into launching an attack across the Sinai at the Suez Canal. Although he gave several different objectives at different times, ranging from a probing attack to a full-scale liberation of Egypt, his primary objective was most likely simply to cut the Canal. Although an impressive logistical feat, his force was beaten back in early February 1915 and he withdrew to Palestine, leaving a small force behind in the desert. Most of 1915 and early 1916 were spent trying to build up his lines of communications and logistics for a further attempt on the Canal, while balancing the resources needed to secure the coast, counter the British–Indian invasion of Mesopotamia and put down internal unrest, all while Enver Pasha demanded that he release troops and materiel for use on other fronts. From June 1916, he also had to contend with the Arab Revolt. A severe plague of locusts in 1915 greatly added to his shortages, but somehow Djemal managed to make impressive progress in expanding the road and rail network in his area and improving his region's military capabilities.

In a civil role, Djemal became notorious for his harsh treatment of Arab nationalists in Syria and Lebanon, including staging public hangings, and earning the nickname 'Djemal the Butcher'. However, his rule was actually more nuanced and politically astute, providing the velvet glove of incentives and concessions in some areas while imposing his iron fist in others, using whichever techniques were best judged to meet his needs. In some areas, he preserved Armenian populations, but in others, he forced conversions or deportation. Within his area of responsibility, an estimated 150,000 Armenians died.

After the failure of his Second Canal Campaign in 1916, Djemal put his forces onto the defensive in southern Palestine, although active operations continued in his other regions. In September 1917, as the forces of the Yildirim Battle Group gathered in Palestine to conduct a fresh offensive into the Sinai, he was relieved of command of that area, although he retained control of the coast of Palestine and the lines of communications and logistics that supported the Yildirim. He was recalled to Constantinople in June 1918, only to return to Syria in September as the EEF launched its autumn offensive. Unable to stem the British advance, he returned to Constantinople at the end of the war, before travelling to Germany in November 1918. By then in exile, he travelled to Switzerland, and in 1920 to Afghanistan as advisor to the Afghan Royal Army. He was convicted of genocide and atrocities by a Turkish military court in 1919, and sentenced to death *in absentia*. In July 1922, he was in Georgia to negotiate with the Communist forces in Russia on behalf of both the Afghans and the Turks when he was assassinated by members of the Armenian Revolutionary Federation.

Born in 1870, **General Friedrich Freiherr Kress von Kressenstein** was commissioned as an ensign into the Bavarian artillery in 1888. He travelled to Constantinople in January 1914 to join the German Military Mission under Liman von Sanders, receiving a commission as a colonel in the Ottoman Army and taking command of the Field Artillery School. On the outbreak of the war, he was sent to the 4th Army in Syria as a staff officer, and he was appointed Chief of Staff to the 1st Expeditionary Corps, then forming to cross the Sinai and attack the Suez Canal. He organized most of the logistical aspects of the force, including the provision of collapsable and transportable boats that could be easily carried across the desert.

With the failure of the force's attack on the Canal in February 1915, Kressenstein was appointed to lead the Desert Command, which was left behind to harass the defences and lay mines in the Canal. Initially using a mixed force of regulars and irregulars, the latter were soon discharged and his regulars scattered through small posts across the desert. Although occasional sniping and attempts to lay mines (only one of which successfully damaged a ship) were made, generally the rest of 1915 passed quietly as Gallipoli absorbed the bulk of Ottoman resources. However, Kressenstein continued (with Djemal Pasha) to make improvements to the logistics across the region, and he was officially appointed Chief of Staff of the 4th Army in July. In December, he was given command of the nominal 1st Expeditionary Force, which was to start forming to make another attack on the Canal. By April 1916, with only a few thousand men available, Kressenstein made either a reconnaissance in force or (more likely) an attempt to establish a forward base in the Qatia region, inflicting heavy casualties on a British Yeomanry brigade. However, being unable to hold the ground, he had to withdraw back to the eastern edge of the desert.

Friedrich Freiherr Kress von Kressenstein looked every inch the austere Teutonic officer, but his relations with his subordinates were often tempestuous.

He returned with a much larger force in July 1916, taking advantage of over a year of logistical preparations to attack the EEF at Romani in August 1916. Defeated, he decided upon establishing a new defensive line between Gaza and Beersheba, and began a skilful fighting retreat across the desert. By January 1917 his new line was established, and, newly promoted to major-general in the Ottoman Army, he successfully defeated British attacks on Gaza in March and April 1917. He continued to develop his defences, and in September 1917, was presented with the Pour le Mérite by the Kaiser. In October, Kressenstein was named commander of the 8th Army, although he was experiencing increasing friction with his new superior, Field Marshal von Falkenhayn, commander of the Yildirim of which the 8th Army was a part. Problems between the two men continued as the EEF launched the Third Battle of Gaza on 31 October 1917, breaking through the Ottoman lines and advancing on Jerusalem. In December 1917, he was removed from his command, and in January 1918, he resigned from the Ottoman Army, reverting to his Bavarian rank of colonel. After returning to Germany, he was appointed to the Caucasus Front in Georgia in June, fighting the Red Army.

After the war, Kressenstein returned to Bavaria and held a succession of staff jobs, eventually reaching the rank of general of artillery in 1928. He retired from the army at the end of 1929, and died in 1948.

BRITISH

Lieutenant-General Sir Archibald Murray was a distinguished and experienced officer who suffered through early 1916 with constantly changing parameters to his command. Born in 1860, he was commissioned in 1879 and attended the Staff College at Camberley in 1897. On graduating, he served as an intelligence officer on the staff of the commander of the forces in Natal during the Boer War, taking battlefield command of those forces with great skill when his seniors were killed. Promoted for his battlefield performance, he commanded a battalion in India before returning to South Africa. There, he was wounded in action and received the Distinguished Service Order. In 1912, he was appointed Inspector of Infantry for the army.

On the outbreak of World War I, Murray was appointed Chief of Staff for the British Expeditionary Force in France, until ill health forced him to return to Britain in January 1915. He was then appointed Deputy to the Chief of the Imperial General Staff (CIGS) with responsibility for training the New Armies being raised by Lord Kitchener. In September 1915, he began a short period as CIGS, the most senior officer in the British Army, but his time was mired in politics and he was relieved in December. Along the way, he was instrumental in laying the groundwork for the introduction of conscription and establishing a 'Westerner' (that is, Western Front-centric) strategy for the war.

Sir Archibald Murray was theatre commander for the entire region, and often unable to give his full attention to just the Sinai Desert. (Universal History Archive/UIG/Getty Images)

In January 1916, Murray was posted to Egypt. On the night of 8/9 January 1916, the MEF had completed its evacuation of the Gallipoli Peninsula. Murray was to take command of the MEF's scattered forces, some already back in Egypt and others based on islands around the Aegean, and all other troops in Egypt except those dedicated to the defence of the Western Desert or the Nile Valley. For the time being, these latter remained under General Sir John Maxwell, who commanded the Egypt defences and oversaw the Martial Law imposed on the county at the start of the war. Murray did have command of the forces in the Sinai Desert.

Murray's command was broad, scattered and confused. The last of the MEF would not arrive in Egypt until February, where most of it became the Imperial Strategic Reserve, ready for deployment anywhere in the world. Over the coming months, one division was sent to Mesopotamia and most of the others to France. He also had initial command of the British Salonika Forces (BSF), but very quickly lost operational command. He did, however, maintain administrative command of the BSF, including logistics, communications and supervision of the rear areas. He also had certain logistical responsibilities for the forces in Mesopotamia and East Africa, along with Cyprus and the Aegean Islands (from April when the Royal Naval Division withdrew). Throughout this period, there was a constant changing of senior commanders and forces within his different commands.

In March 1916, the situation was simplified somewhat as all of the forces in Egypt were unified under Murray's command, although this also left him with a range of responsibilities for the civil administration of the country as well. The EEF was created, consisting of four infantry divisions, one mounted division and multiple independent mounted brigades, while the rest of the old MEF continued to be posted to France. Murray has been criticized in some quarters for his detached approach to the campaign in the Sinai, but this was more than understandable given his wide-reaching responsibilities. He could no more focus entirely on the advance across the Sinai than he could on the road networks of Salonika or the camps on Mudros. He was a theatre commander for the entire eastern Mediterranean, and Egypt was just one part of his responsibilities.

In early 1917, Murray would become more focused on the EEF and its advance into Palestine. His actions during the First and Second Battles of Gaza in March and April 1917, and his disingenuous reporting of them back to the War Office, would lead to his being removed from command in June 1917. In 1919, he was appointed General Officer Commanding of the Aldershot Garrison, which he held until his retirement in 1922. Sir Archibald Murray died in 1945.

Major-General the Honourable Sir Herbert Lawrence was born in 1861, and commissioned into the British Army in 1882. He graduated from the Staff College in 1896, and during the Boer War worked in an intelligence role, being twice Mentioned in Despatches and finishing the war as a lieutenant colonel. He resigned his commission in 1903 to enter business, although from 1904–09, he also served as an officer in King Edward's Horse, a London-based Yeomanry regiment. Recalled to the colours in 1914, he was placed on the staff of the 2nd Yeomanry Division and embarked with them to Egypt in March 1915. In June, he was transferred to take command of the 127th (Manchester) Brigade, in the 42nd (East Lancashire) Division in the Dardanelles, and in July was sent to Mudros to overhaul the struggling communications systems, which were breaking down under the strain of the campaign. In September, he was promoted again to command the 52nd (Lowland) Division, also serving at Gallipoli. When Cape Helles was evacuated, he was one of the last men off the beach.

After the division's withdrawal to Egypt and its reorganization in early 1916, the 52nd Division joined the Suez Canal defences and then formed part of the new EEF. Lawrence was given command of No. 3 Section Canal Defences – the most northerly stretch. This was a corps-sized command, encompassing not only the Canal defences but also the advanced parties that were being sent out to establish the forward defences,

Sir Herbert Lawrence was the commander of the British forces in the northern Sinai for most of 1916, although he is better remembered now for his later work on Sir Douglas Haig's staff on the Western Front in 1918. (© National Portrait Gallery, London)

first at Qatia and later Romani. As such, Lawrence commanded the EEF's forces at the Battle of Romani in August 1916, and the initial pursuit of the Ottoman forces. Soon after the battle, he asked to be relieved and sent back to the UK for personal reasons, and he was given command of the 71st Division in England. In February 1917, he was given command of the 66th Division, and he took the unit to France a short time later. In October 1917, Lawrence took over the intelligence staff at GHQ in France, and in early 1918 became General Haig's Chief of Staff. In this role, he played a vital but unsung role in smoothing Anglo-French relations during the spring and summer, notably during the negotiations to form a supreme allied command on the Western Front.

Lawrence resigned his commission again in 1919, although he retained links with the army and became a Trustee of the Imperial (now Commonwealth) War Graves Commission in 1925. He enjoyed a successful business career, and died in 1943.

Born in 1865, **Major-General Sir Harry Chauvel** joined the Upper Clarence Light Horse Regiment when it was raised by his father in 1886. Determined upon a regular military career, he accepted a captaincy on the Queensland military staff in 1896. The following year he travelled to England with the Australian contingent for Queen Victoria's Diamond Jubilee celebrations, and then remained for a year serving with the British Army. In 1899, he commanded two companies of the Queensland Mounted Infantry when it embarked for the Boer War, later taking command of a regiment as a major. At the end of his one year's service in South Africa, he returned home, and in 1902, as a lieutenant colonel, landed again in Durban as commander of the 7th Commonwealth Light Horse in time for the last few weeks of the war. He remained in the new, small regular Australian Army after the war and played a crucial part in raising and training the Light Horse units of the part-time Citizen Military Force. From 1911, he undertook staff work, and in 1914, he was sent to the UK to be the Australian representative on the Imperial General Staff.

Chauvel was still en route when war broke out, and he was given command of the 1st Light Horse Brigade. He trained the force in Egypt and led it to Gallipoli in May 1915. In November 1915, he was appointed temporary commander of the 1st Australian Division, a command made permanent with the rank of major-general the following month. After the withdrawal from Gallipoli to Egypt, Chauvel was given command of the newly formed Australian and New Zealand (A&NZ) Mounted Division in March 1916. This force formed part of the No. 3 Section Canal Defences, and his troops provided a crucial long-range reconnaissance ability for the EEF. From June 1916, Chauvel's duties stretched

Sir Henry 'Light Horse Harry' Chauvel had a dashing reputation, but remained always conscious of the logistical problems involved in campaigning in the desert, and the effects on the health of his horses and men. (Australian War Memorial J00503)

beyond his existing battlefield command as he was appointed the Force Commander for all Australian troops in Egypt. Reporting to Lieutenant-General Birdwood in France, Chauvel (much like Murray) found himself responsible for a wide range of services outside his immediate command, including the medical facilities, administrative services, and air and support units for the Australian forces in the region.

At the Battle of Romani in August 1916, his division took the brunt of the initial Ottoman attacks, and afterwards formed the bulk of the pursuit forces. Near the end of the campaign, Chauvel's division formed the larger part of the strike forces that attacked isolated Ottoman outposts on the eastern side of the Sinai Desert. In 1917, he led his division during the First and Second Battles of Gaza, and the raiding and patrolling on the EEF's desert flank over the summer. In August 1917, the cavalry forces of the EEF were grouped together as the Desert Mounted Corps (DMC), and Chauvel was promoted to lieutenant-general and given command of it – the first Australian to permanently command a corps-sized formation. He led the DMC with great success during the Third Battle of Gaza and advance to Jerusalem from October–December 1917, and again during the 1918 campaigns in the Jordan Valley, northern Palestine and Syria. He was frequently given considerable independence by the EEF's commander.

In 1919, Chauvel returned to Australia and became Inspector General of the Australian Army, and in 1923, became the Chief of Staff. He retired in 1930, and died in 1945.

A signals section from the Norfolk Yeomanry display some of their equipment, including flags and heliographs.

OPPOSING FORCES

OTTOMAN

The Ottoman Army in the Sinai Desert in 1916 was a changing and often ad hoc organization. The need to concentrate on the Gallipoli campaign in 1915, support the campaigns in Mesopotamia and (from June 1916) counter the outbreak of revolt in the Arab Peninsula, meant that the force was constantly changing and seldom properly supplied. The Ottoman Empire's industrial base was small, and much of the ordnance, munitions and other supplies required had to make a long trip from their European allies across Eastern Europe, Anatolia, and down the length of Syria and Palestine. The route was long and necessitated changing between boats, trains and trucks many times. The wastage rate was high, and delays and shortages were the norm.

For the average Ottoman soldier, this often meant subsistence on poor food and only the most rudimentary of medical care. Most soldiers were drawn from the peasant classes; illiterate, uneducated and often lacking in initiative, they were also tough, courageous and, when properly led,

Ottoman forces defend trenches in the eastern Sinai. Despite lacking material such as barbed wire, Ottoman troops were excellent at siting and defending trenches.

determined in both the attack and the defence. They showed particular skill in the siting of defensive positions, using the ground to great advantage. Their lack of barbed wire and other reinforcing materials was compensated for by their ability to blend into the landscape. After the border battles of December 1916 and January 1917, Brigadier-General Sir Guy Dawnay, Chief of Staff of the Eastern Force, visited the sites of the defences at both Magdhaba and El Magruntein. At Magdhaba, the Ottoman 'works around the place were the most cunningly sited I have ever seen. You can't see them at all till you absolutely walk into them. Our artillery could never pick them up'. At El Magruntein, he found 'a splendidly selected position on a small rise in a gently rolling, grassy plain; absolute "glacis" slopes all round – not a mouse could move up to attack it without being seen from ever so far'.

The average Ottoman soldier could subsist on poor-quality rations (although this tended to put further strain on already inadequate medical services) and drink water from desert wells that the British had deemed undrinkable. Discipline tended to be harsh, and the levels of training varied across the army. Different national or cultural groupings within the army were perceived in different ways, with the Christians and Jews (both previously exempt from service) called up at the outbreak of the war soon being relegated to labour battalions, while Arab troops were treated with mistrust despite their consistently high performance.

Each man wore a khaki uniform similar to their adversary, and a 'kabalak' hat, designed by Enver Pasha (and so was also known as an 'enveriye'), which consisted of a frame around which two long strips of fabric were wound to make the cover. Each man was equipped with a rifle – most commonly an 1893 or 1903 pattern bolt-action, magazine-feed 7.65mm Mauser, although older single-shot weapons, including Peabody-Martini breech-loaders, were also in service. Each man carried 130 rounds of ammunition and a bayonet.

The basic Ottoman infantry formation was the regiment, consisting of four battalions (numbered 1st to 4th) which usually served together. Each consisted of four companies of four officers and 260 men, a small battalion headquarters and a machine-gun section. Three regiments plus an artillery regiment, a cavalry squadron, a pioneers (engineers) company and a sanitation company made up an infantry division with a full-strength of 10,000–12,000 men. Three divisions, along with an artillery and a cavalry regiment, would make a corps. Although no units of this size could be supported in the Sinai, the Ottoman defences in southern Palestine were of corps-strength.

The Ottomans did not have large regular cavalry formations in the Sinai until the end of the campaign, but each cavalry regiment had four front-line squadrons of 130 officers and men, plus a regimental headquarters of 30 officers and men. The cavalry was armed with carbines and swords or lances. Artillery was also often in short supply in the desert, due to the logistics involved in moving and supporting the guns. An artillery regiment, as attached to an infantry division, had either two or three battalions, each consisting of three batteries of four field guns. The guns were of foreign manufacture and came in a variety of calibres, but as the war progressed, German or Austro-Hungarian types became standard, such as the Krupps 75mm field gun or 105mm or 150mm howitzers. Mountain guns were also used in the desert. These could be broken down into several parts and carried on mules or camels and so were easier to transport, but were smaller in calibre and had less range.

All of the above strengths were nominal, and units were frequently below their full establishment due to sickness, desertion or simple demographics. The Ottoman Empire operated a system of conscription, but had a relatively small population compared to the size of its land mass. From 1915 onwards, year on year Ottoman casualties would exceed the numbers being called up, and the army was fated to shrink accordingly.

Trained officers were also usually in short supply (partly due to the educational standards required) and Ottoman officers often commanded units one or even two levels higher than would be expected of their British counterparts. Some of this shortage was made up with German officers from the German Military Mission under the direction of General Liman von Sanders. This German assistance was very much a mixed blessing. The Military Mission had arrived in Constantinople in late 1913, when the Ottomans were reeling from defeats in the Balkans Wars. However, those recent conflicts meant that the average Ottoman officer had considerably more combat experience than the German officers who were now arriving. The Germans as a rule treated the Ottomans with a level of contempt, and few bothered to learn Arabic. Even Kress von Kressenstein exhibited in his diaries constantly patronizing and dismissive attitudes towards his Ottoman officers and men, and he was one of the more enlightened Germans. Friction was inevitable, and while some Germans did go on to make significant contributions, overall the mix of languages, cultures and training styles added little to Ottoman fighting efficiency.

Ottoman officers rest in their tent before the Battle of Romani. (Trustees of the Queen's Own Worcestershire Hussars Museum)

Of more use were the specialist troops that the Germans and Austro-Hungarians sent to Palestine. Known as 'Pasha Force' (and later, after further contingents were sent, 'Pasha 1'), this force consisted of a machine-gun battalion (eight companies) and four heavy artillery batteries, but also (importantly for the logistically challenged Ottomans) signals, motor-transport, bridging, catering and medical units. Crucially, the Pasha Force included a single flying detachment, Flieger Abteilung 300 (FA300). This flying unit only included a front-line strength of eight aeroplanes – six reconnaissance/bomber Rumpler C.1s and two fighter Pfalz E.IIs – but these aircraft outclassed the available British aircraft, which were too few in number to effectively control the air over the Sinai anyway. The forward detachment of FA300 arrived in April 1916 and within days provided vital intelligence to Kressenstein.

Most of the German troops would not arrive until the early summer, and the lack of time to acclimatize before being sent into the Sinai in the heat of the season had a considerable effect on their efficiency, as did the lack of supplies. For example, the War Diary of the 605th Machine Gun Company (now held by the Australian War Memorial) records that one officer and 31 NCOs and other ranks left Constantinople on 30 April and only arrived at Beersheba on 2 June, having used horses, trucks and several different trains along the way. During the journey, some of the ammunition boxes had been so poorly handled that the cartridges had been damaged and a high rate of stoppages were experienced. Once at Beersheba, the company received 75 Ottoman troops to be trained on their machine guns. After only a month, on 6 July, the company (reduced to 25 Germans through sickness

The Rumpler C.1s of FA300 were of disproportionate importance in the Sinai campaign. Few in number, they were able to outclass British and Australian aircraft and could establish local air superiority.

but still with 74 Ottomans) was marched into the desert, where they suffered from lack of water and the poor quality of the Ottoman rations. As with the Germans across the Expeditionary Force, they also struggled to effectively communicate with their Ottoman comrades. The Pasha Force totalled 140 officers and 1,500 men.

Small numbers of irregular troops were used by the Ottomans, but only for short periods. After the failure of the February 1915 attack on the Suez Canal, Kressenstein had been left with the Desert Command, containing a mix of regular and irregular troops to hold the Sinai. One irregular force was the Hedjaz Camel Regiment (also known as 'raiders'), which fought in the attack in April 1916, but after the outbreak of the Arab Revolt in June 1916 was despatched as part of the reinforcements sent to Medina. A fluctuating number of local Bedouin volunteers also served in the Desert Command, but such forces were always viewed with suspicion by the Ottomans and saw limited use.

BRITISH

The British and Imperial forces in the Sinai desert in 1916 were drawn principally from Great Britain, Australia and New Zealand with small numbers of Indian troops (but will be referred to by default as 'British', as the forces of the British Empire). There were no regular British Army front-line units in the EEF, which was formed in March 1916. The vast majority were units of the Territorial Forces, or the Australian and New Zealand equivalents; part-time soldiers whose companies, squadrons and battalions were generally drawn from a small and distinct geographical area. This gave each unit a strong and distinctive identity, and service at Gallipoli had imbued them with experience and pride. Although losses at Gallipoli had been high, as a rule losses were made up from recruits from the same areas. The introduction of the Military Service Act in England, Scotland and Wales in January 1916 would gradually see those connections become diluted across the British Army as a whole; men conscripted under the Act would increasingly be simply posted to where they were needed regardless of county or city connections. However, this was less of an issue in the EEF, given the relatively low casualty rates in the 1916 campaign, and these strong identities and resulting *esprit de corps* remained strong in most units throughout the campaign. New Zealand would follow suit in implementing conscription in August 1916, although 75 per cent of their recruits continued to be volunteers, while in Australia, two referenda on conscription in 1916 saw the move rejected. In Ireland, conscription was deemed too politically contentious.

All British Imperial troops were dressed in khaki uniforms of a broadly similar design; some differences existed between the different arms, or with the Scottish regiments, while the Australians also wore slightly different uniforms. As a rule, the biggest difference between national contingents was the headgear, such as the Scottish glengarry cap, the Australian slouch-hat and the New Zealand 'lemon squeezer' hat. The standard British headgear was the pith helmet, with multiple designs in use, but even this broad rule had its limitations. Some Australian units were temporarily issued pith helmets, while some British troops wore slouch-hats, and individual men of all units

Men of the 10th Battalion Manchester Regiment patrol in the Sinai, searching and escorting local inhabitants.

sometimes preferred peaked caps. In the desert, dress regulations were lax and the men were generally allowed to adopt or adapt what was comfortable and functional to a large degree, although this could lead to friction with the local military authorities on the rare occasions leave passes could be obtained to return to Cairo or Alexandria.

All were equipped with the same standard long arm, the .303in calibre Short Magazine Lee–Enfield (SMLE) rifle. The type was rugged and accurate, and came with a bayonet. British Yeomanry units also carried the 1908-pattern sword, a superbly balanced weapon designed primarily for thrusting. Infantry and mounted units were also equipped with machine guns. 'Heavy' Vickers machine guns were operated by a four-man crew and were concentrated in battalion or regiment level units, enabling them to be deployed where most needed. Increasingly, companies and squadrons were receiving 'light' machine guns, with two-man crews. Eventually, the infantry would become standardized with Lewis guns, and the cavalry with the French Hotchkiss Gun Mk. 1, although in 1916, shortages of both types led to whatever types were available being issued wherever they were needed.

The basic infantry unit was the battalion, made up of four companies of just over 200 officers and men, plus a headquarters (including signallers, clerks and medical staff) and a machine-gun unit. Each company consisted of four platoons, each divided into four sections. Each battalion belonged to a larger regiment, but the regiments themselves were not battlefield organizations. Instead, four battalions (regardless of parent regiment) would be grouped together to form a brigade, although as a legacy of their Territorial Force origins, several brigades in the EEF were drawn entirely from single regiments. Three brigades (plus supporting troops) would form a division.

The artillery came in several types, depending on size and function. The Royal Horse Artillery (RHA) were lighter, with 13-pdr Quick Firing (QF) guns. They were for battlefield use, able to gallop into close range, deploy and then gallop quickly away again if needed. The RHA (which included the Honourable Artillery Company – HAC) were attached to the mounted forces. The Royal Field Artillery (RFA) had larger, heavier and less mobile guns. Using a mix of 18-pdr QF Guns and 4.5in howitzers, these units had longer ranges and were attached to the infantry divisions.

For the Sinai campaign, the mounted troops would be the EEF's most active forces, scouting, patrolling and acting as long-range strike forces. These came in several types. The British Yeomanry, Australian Light Horse and New Zealand Mounted Rifles were all technically 'mounted riflemen', organized like cavalry into regiments of three squadrons of around 150 men each, plus a headquarters and machine-gun squadron. They were primarily intended to ride into battle and then dismount to fight on foot, with one man in four holding the horses. Their comparative lack of firepower was compensated for by their mobility. On occasion, they could fight from horseback, although the British Yeomanry were the only ones to carry actual swords. Three cavalry regiments would be grouped together to make a brigade, and three or four brigades to make a division, although the cavalry units much more frequently operated in smaller units as they scouted the desert and harassed the enemy. A single Indian cavalry brigade, the Imperial Service Cavalry Brigade, served in the Canal zone, with three regiments of lancers.

Mounted troops rest. Although each nationality had its own uniform and equipment distinctions, it was not uncommon to see them being mixed. These men wear Australian Light Horse slouch hats but are using British Yeomanry rifle holsters, which were not issued to the Australians.

Cavalry could act as scouts, as rapidly deployable reinforcements or as shock troops. Their main strength was in their ability to move fast over long distances, and they would generally provide the main striking force of the EEF in 1916. Equally, the need to water the horses, who would rapidly lose their strength and health after 24 hours or more without a drink, was often the main limiting factor on the EEF's abilities. As such a crucial part of the EEF, it is worth taking a look at the equipment carried, as described by Lieutenant A. Briscoe Moore of the New Zealand Mounted Rifles:

> The load carried by a Mounted Rifleman's horse in the field is considerable, and may be described here in some detail, to give the reader some idea of what is required of these horses in endurance. The description given is of the minimum load ... consisting of bare essentials only.
>
> The Mounted Rifleman wore, on his person, a leather bandolier containing 90 rounds of ammunition, bayonet, service rifle, and haversack, the latter usually stuffed with tins of the inevitable 'bully' beef and army biscuits. The saddlery on his mount consisted of headstall and bridle, headrope, picketing rope, saddle and blanket. In addition to this the horse carried, slung around his neck, a leather sand muzzle, which was slipped on in place of the nosebag when he had finished his meagre feed, to prevent him eating sand and dirt; this being a bad habit quickly indulged in by many horses when hungry.
>
> In this sand-muzzle the trooper often carried his mess-tin, or 'billy' for cooking or making tea, and his dandy brush for grooming. The next item was the horse bandolier, slung around the horse's neck and containing an additional 90 rounds of ammunition. Strapped on the front of the saddle were two leather wallets, probably containing towel, soap, spare shirt, socks, and what rations the rider could not get into his haversack; strapped on top of these again would be the greatcoat and one blanket.
>
> The men usually set out with forty-eight hours' rations and an iron ration, while the horse ration for three days (27 lbs) would be carried. This horsefeed would be distributed between two nosebags, tied to the side of the saddle, and a sandbag, round which might be rolled a ground or bivouac sheet, strapped across the rear of the saddle. Also slung to the side of the saddle would be the canvas water-bucket which served the soldier for the watering of his horse and his own ablutions, and his water-bottle.

The Imperial Camel Corps (ICC) was also expanded during 1916. These camel-mounted troops were drawn from volunteers from the other cavalry units, but were organized as 'mounted infantry', in companies of 200 men. Of the three battalions formed in 1916, the 1st (Australian) and 3rd (Australian) each had four companies, while the 2nd (British) Battalion had six companies. Two independent companies of New Zealand Cameliers were also formed (and with two Australian companies formed into a 4th Battalion in 1917). The units were generally used at platoon or company strength for patrolling, raiding and scouting, although they would be formed into ad hoc full battalions for major actions, and several battalions could be formed into an ad hoc brigade, with a permanent Imperial Camel Corps Brigade being established in 1917. Again, they generally rode into action and then dismounted to fight, although occasional mounted actions did occur.

Britain's flying services in Egypt, the 5th Wing Royal Flying Corps (RFC), usually consisted of two squadrons. No. 14 Squadron remained throughout

1916, and No. 17 Squadron served until being despatched to Salonika in July. No. 1 Squadron Australian Flying Corps (AFC) had arrived in April, but due to the lack of adequate training facilities in Australia, had to be broken up for further training, reforming and becoming operational in July. Their primary equipment was the Royal Aircraft Factory BE2c, although a few newer types did begin to arrive in 1916, and they were used for scouting and bombing in the Western and Sinai deserts. They enjoyed a numerical advantage but were at a technological disadvantage against FA300. However, the numbers of aircraft over the Sinai were so small that air-to-air combat was rare.

A small French seaplane unit, the Port Said Seaplane Squadron, had been operating off the Sinai and Palestine coasts since 1914, and while it had made extremely valuable contributions in 1915, its aircraft were badly outdated by 1916, and it was withdrawn during the spring. It was replaced by the East Indies and Egypt Seaplane Squadron (EI&ESS) of the Royal Naval Air Service (RNAS). Its aircraft were floatplanes, two-seat Short 184s and single-seat Sopwith Schneiders or Sopwith Babys, and operated from the converted ferries HMS *Ben-My-Chree* and HMS *Empress*, and from the captured German merchantmen HMS *Raven II* and HMS *Anne*. Its main role was reconnaissance, although it also spotted for the guns of various French or Royal Navy ships offshore to attack coastal defences and infrastructure. Flat-bottomed monitors, each armed with a single large calibre and several smaller guns, were used to move close inshore for such work, as was the sloop HMS *Espiegle*.

Although not technically troops, the men of the Egyptian Labour Corps (ELC) also deserve mention as a critical part of the British forces. Indeed, without the ELC, the EEF would not have been able to progress across the Sinai at the same rate. Thousands of Egyptians volunteered (at this point in the war, in 1917, conscription was imposed) to serve for three-month tours with the ELC or its sub-unit, the Camel Transport Corps (CTC). Instituted in

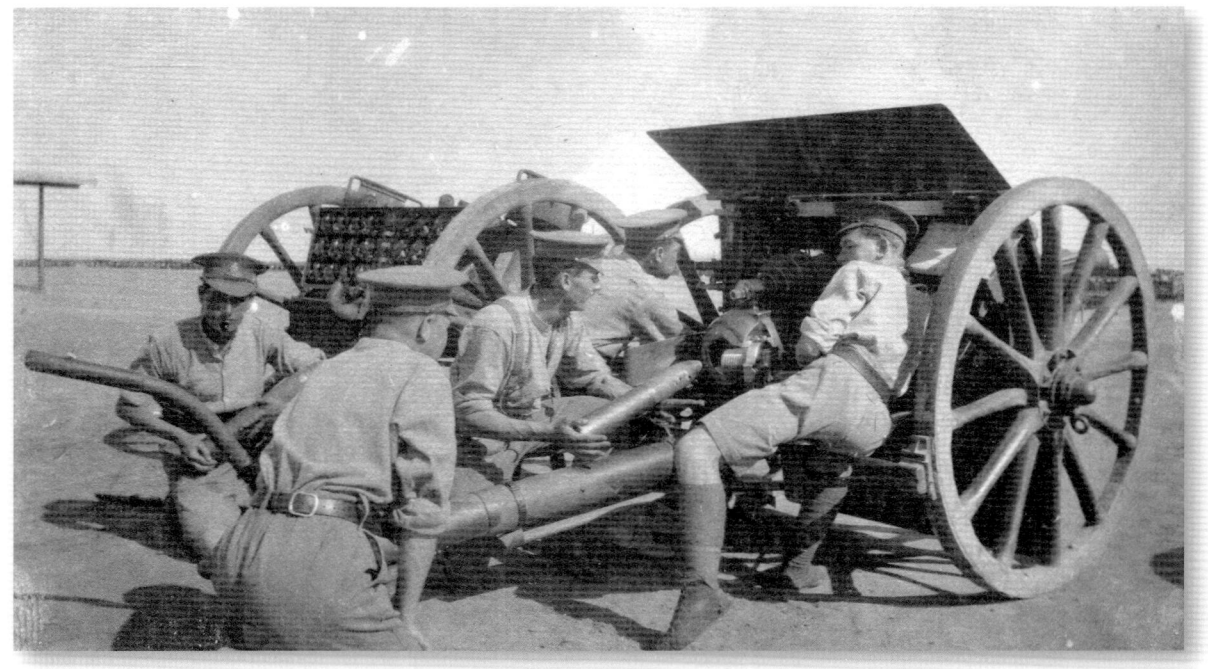

A British 13-pdr QF gun. Artillery played a much smaller role in the Sinai than in other World War I campaigns. Their heavy guns, wagons and the necessary horse teams were often hard to move or supply in the desert.

January 1916 with a strength of 500 men, by the end of the year they had risen to over 40,000 members. They acted as labourers and herdsmen, laying both the railway and the pipeline across the desert, as well as keeping the camel convoys moving, digging wells, unloading boats and all manner of other manual work. Others did more technical jobs, including in ordnance or in instrument and tool repairs. Discipline was harsh, often under British or Imperial officers and NCOs who spoke little Arabic and communicated through physical means instead, but the pay was good. Small numbers of these Egyptians also served overseas in the Dardanelles, Mesopotamia, Malta, Salonika and France. Their contribution was considerable and often overlooked.

ORDERS OF BATTLE

AFFAIR AT QATIA, APRIL 1916

OTTOMAN FORCES

1st Expeditionary Corps
Colonel Kress von Kressenstein

1st Battalion 32nd Regiment
2nd Battalion 32nd Regiment
One company 3rd Battalion 32nd Regiment
One squadron of Ottoman regular camel troops (Halid Bey)
Hedjaz Camel Regiment (Major Carl Muhlmann)
Six mountain guns
75mm battery 8th Field Artillery Regiment (four guns)
Half battery 9th Field Artillery Regiment (two guns)
Two field ambulances
Ammunition column

BRITISH AND IMPERIAL FORCES

No. 3 Canal Section
Major-General the Hon. Sir Herbert Lawrence

5th Mounted Brigade
Colonel (temp. Brigadier-General) E. A. Wiggin
1/1st Warwickshire Yeomanry
1/1st Royal Gloucestershire Hussars (Yeomanry)
1/1st Queen's Own Worcestershire Hussars (Yeomanry)
413th Field Squadron, Royal Engineers

1/4th & 1/5th Battalions Royal Scots Fusiliers
Queen's Own Royal Glasgow Yeomanry
Bikaner Camel Corps
5th Regiment Australian Light Horse

BATTLE OF ROMANI, 4–5 AUGUST 1916

OTTOMAN FORCES

Fourth Army
Djemal Pasha

1st Expeditionary Force
Colonel Kress von Kressenstein

3rd Infantry Division
Colonel Refet Bele

31st Infantry Regiment (Lieutenant Colonel Ismail Hakki Bey)
1st, 2nd, 3rd & 4th Battalions

32nd Infantry Regiment (Lieutenant Colonel Hasan Basri Bey; from 5 August Lieutenant Colonel Ibrahim Bey)
1st, 2nd, 3rd & 4th Battalions

39th Infantry Regiment (Lieutenant Colonel Nurettin Bey; from 4 August Major Kamil Bey)
1st, 2nd, 3rd & 4th Battalions

Attached Troops
2nd Independent Camel Company (Lieutenant Colonel Bischof)
2nd Battalion 81st Infantry Regiment
3rd Regiment of Mountain Artillery
32nd Machine Gun Company
1/1st, 4/2nd & 1/5th Engineer Companies

German Units
601st, 602nd, 603rd, 604th, 605th, 606th, 607th & 608th Machine Gun Companies
60th Battalion Heavy Artillery

Austrian Units
No. 9 Mortar Battery
No. 36 Howitzer Battery

BRITISH AND IMPERIAL FORCES

No. 3 Canal Section
Major-General the Hon. Sir Herbert Lawrence

Australian and New Zealand Mounted Division
Colonel (temp. Major-General) H. G. Chauvel

1st Australian Light Horse Brigade (Lieutenant Colonel John Meredith; vice Lieutenant Colonel Charles Cox)
1st, 2nd & 3rd Australian Light Horse Regiments

2nd Australian Light Horse Brigade (Colonel John Royston; vice Colonel G. de L. Ryrie)
6th & 7th Australian Light Horse Regiments
Wellington Mounted Rifles Regiment

42nd (East Lancashire) Division (Major-General Sir W. Douglas)

125th Infantry Brigade (Colonel (temp. Brigadier-General) H. C. Frith)
1/5th, 1/6th, 1/7th & 1/8th Battalions Lancashire Fusiliers
125th Brigade Machine Gun Company

126th Infantry Brigade (Major (temp. Brigadier-General) A. W. Tufnell)
1/4th & 1/5th Battalions East Lancashire Regiment
1/9th & 1/10th Battalions Manchester Regiment
126th Brigade Machine Gun Company

127th Infantry Brigade (Lieutenant Colonel (temp. Brigadier-General) V. A. Ormsby)
1/5th, 1/6th, 1/7th & 1/8th Battalions Manchester Regiment
127th Brigade Machine Gun Company

52nd (Lowland) Division (General W. E. B. Smith; vice Major-General Lawrence)

155th Infantry Brigade (Lieutenant Colonel (temp. Brigadier-General) J. B. Pollok-McCall)
1/4th & 1/5th Battalions Royal Scots Fusiliers
1/4th & 1/5th Battalions King's Own Scottish Borderers
155th Brigade Machine Gun Company

156th Infantry Brigade (Brevet Colonel (temp. Brigadier-General) L. C. Koe)
1/4th & 1/7th Battalions Royal Scots
1/7th & 1/8th Battalions Scottish Rifles
156th Brigade Machine Gun Company

157th Infantry Brigade (Brevet Colonel (temp. Brigadier-General) H. G. Casson)
1/5th, 1/6th & 1/7th Battalions Highland Light Infantry
1/5th Battalion Argyll and Sutherland Highlanders
157th Brigade Machine Gun Company

158th Infantry Brigade (attached from 53rd Division) (Major (temp. Brigadier-General) S. F. Mott)
1/5th, 1/6th & 1/7th Battalions Royal Welch Fusiliers
1/1st Battalion Herefordshire Regiment
158th Brigade Machine Gun Company

3rd Australian Light Horse Brigade (General John Antill)
8th, 9th & 10th Australian Light Horse Regiments

Sector Mounted Troops (Brigadier-General E. W. C. Chaytor)

New Zealand Mounted Rifles Brigade
Auckland & Canterbury Mounted Rifles Regiments
5th Australian Light Horse Regiment

5th Mounted Brigade (Colonel (temp. Brigadier-General) E. A. Wiggin)
1/1st Warwickshire Yeomanry
Composite Regiment (combined remnants of 1/1st Royal Gloucestershire Hussars and 1/1st Queen's Own Worcestershire Hussars)

A British cavalry camp in the Qatia region. The horse lines in such camps were extremely vulnerable to artillery or air attack.

OPPOSING PLANS

OTTOMAN

The Ottomans had entered World War I without any clear war aims. Their involvement was reluctant, even after signing a treaty with Germany in August 1914. After months of quibbling and delay, the Germans forced their hands by orchestrating an Ottoman naval attack on Russia at the end of October. Objectives involving the recapture of areas lost to the Russians in the Caucasus in the 1870s and the liberation of Egypt from the British were soon improvised, but lack of strategic cohesion would be a constant issue for the Ottomans throughout the war. The plan to liberate Egypt initially manifested itself as a multi-division advance across the Sinai Desert in January 1915, assaulting the Suez Canal in early February and being beaten back. The need to defend the Dardanelles absorbed Ottoman attention for most of the rest of 1915, but a small force under the German Colonel Kress von Kressenstein (initially of mixed regulars and irregulars, but later only regular troops) remained in the Sinai to harass the British. With the end of the Dardanelles campaign and under German pressure to force Britain to keep as many troops in Egypt as possible, the Ottomans formed the 1st Expeditionary Force, but were obliged to deploy it far sooner than they wanted, in April 1916. Kressenstein gathered a small column with the intent of establishing a forward operating base in the Qatia area, and although this was briefly seized in late April, it could not be held.

It would take until July for the Expeditionary Force to gather another, much larger army and for the logistical preparations needed to supply it in the Sinai to be completed. This was again aimed at the

As this German propaganda poster shows, the ultimate Ottoman goal was to liberate Egypt and push the British out of the country.

The western Sinai Desert and the Qatia basin, 1916

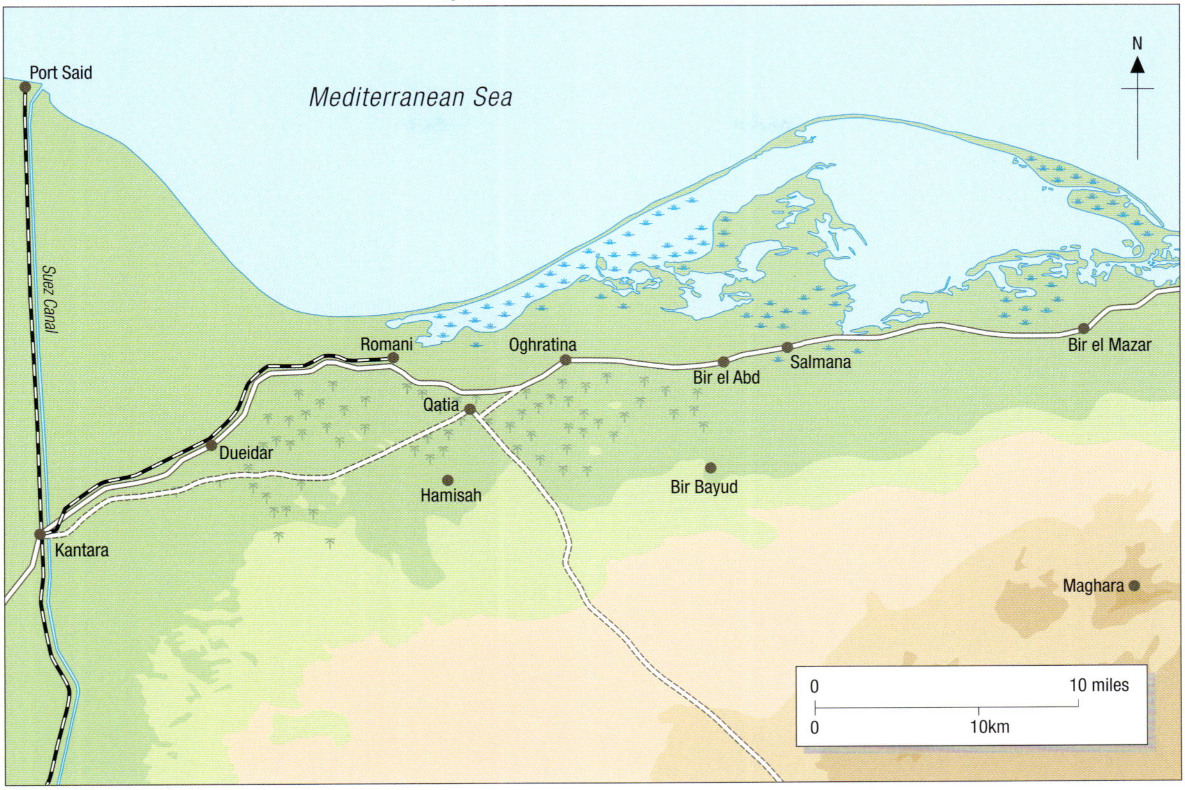

Qatia area, and at the known British positions just north-west of Qatia at Romani. Kressenstein planned to pin down the main British line from the front while the bulk of his forces swept around the southern flank, cutting off the advanced British units and destroying their logistical support. After capturing or forcing out the British advanced posts, he would establish a base in the area from which to apply constant pressure to the Suez Canal.

After the Ottoman defeat at Romani in early August, it became clear that this plan was untenable and that any forces left in the desert would themselves be vulnerable to British attack. Kressenstein began a steady, well-organized fighting retreat across the Sinai. There would be considerable debate among the Ottoman high command over whether to abandon the Sinai completely. On the one hand, there were the political and propaganda implications of withdrawing from Egypt, and the logistical repercussions of abandoning the considerable investments that had been made in the infrastructure. On the other, the Ottomans could not afford to lose more men or materiel in defending worthless desert. The decision

In the shorter term, Ottoman plans centred on building up the logistics necessary to campaign in the Sinai, including extending the rail network. Here is the station at Beersheba. (Library of Congress Prints and Photographs Division)

to finally withdraw was made in early December, although Ottoman garrisons would remain in the desert until the end of the year. These were mostly intended to delay the British advance only, allowing time for a new defensive line to be established just north of the border with Palestine, between Gaza on the coast and Beersheba some 45km (30 miles) inland, with a logistical hub at Tel el Sharia roughly half-way between them.

BRITISH

On the outbreak of conflict, Britain had attempted to delay war in the Middle East for as long as possible. The Ottoman Sultan was also the Caliph, the spiritual head of Sunni Islam, and the Entente Powers feared his ability to call for a global jihad (holy war). Both the British and French empires contained far more Muslims than the Ottoman Empire did, and even limited uprisings in India or across Africa could be a major drain on Entente resources. However, Britain also needed to secure the crucial Suez Canal. A delicate balancing act was maintained in Egypt, with fear of civil unrest being weighed against the need to send its regular garrison brigade to France. The Sinai Desert was abandoned as too difficult to defend; any outposts would be too hard to supply, and too easily isolated and destroyed. As half-trained Territorial Forces from the 42nd (East Lancashire) Division and untrained Australian and New Zealand volunteers flowed into the country, a small force of regular Indian Army troops was diverted from the convoys to France to establish a defensive line along the Suez Canal itself.

These forces, supported by British and French warships on the Canal, successfully repulsed the Ottoman attack in February 1915, but it was clear that the current situation was untenable. Throughout 1915, with the military in Egypt focused on supporting the campaign in the Dardanelles or, from November, repulsing the Senussi invasion from Libya across the Western Desert, there were simply no resources available to establish a defensive line deeper

Men of the Norfolk Yeomanry dig in on the Suez Canal. Note the extensive framework needed to keep the trench's shape in the soft sand. A much wider and deeper trench than necessary would be dug, the frame inserted and then the gaps back-filled.

into the desert. However, Sir John Maxwell, commander in Egypt, did begin preparations, starting to construct the logistical framework in terms of water filters, pipelines, roads and railways to support large forces in the Canal zone.

With the withdrawal of the MEF to Egypt, troops were finally available, and, after a period of rest, re-equipping and retraining, the newly created EEF began serious preparations for establishing a forward defence. The Qatia area was chosen. Qatia itself and the surrounding areas had numerous wells, and it stood on the northern caravan road across the Sinai. Of the three main routes across the desert, this was the most likely line of attack. The southern one went through heavily mountainous areas, impassable to artillery and heavy transport, while the central route was also more mountainous and more difficult to cross.

Preparations began in March 1916 to establish positions in the Qatia basin, an area of low-lying ground in the region of Qatia where good water could be found relatively easily at shallow depths. However, the Ottoman attack in April showed that these were too isolated and vulnerable. The EEF instead began to establish significant positions at Romani, to the north-west, while waiting for its logistics (especially the railway) to catch up.

By July, it was clear that the Ottomans were also gathering in the Sinai in strength, with some wild estimates of Ottoman numbers reaching into the hundreds of thousands. Patrols from the Royal Flying Corps and the Mounted Riflemen of the Australian and New Zealand (A&NZ) Mounted Division were monitoring the growth of Ottoman forces, but their intention was unclear. British intelligence judged that they may stage an attack, and 4 August was estimated as the earliest possible date for such an assault. General Lawrence, in consultation with Generals Smith (commanding the 52nd (Lowland) Division) and Chauvel, established a plan, which Murray approved in late July. The 52nd Division was to dig in on high ground to the east of Romani, establishing redoubts along a 4-mile north–south front. It was expected that the Ottomans would try to pass this line to the south, and so to the south of them, a piquet line of the A&NZ Mounted Division would screen the open flank, disrupting any Ottoman advance while swinging back to an east–west line. With the Ottomans drawn into a new, northward-facing attack, British and New Zealand mounted forces, the Imperial Camel Corps Brigade and infantry from the 42nd Division would attack the Ottoman's open left flank, rolling up their line.

Overall, this plan was a success and the Ottoman forces were defeated at the Battle of Romani in August after two days of heavy fighting. A limited pursuit then followed for several more days until Lawrence's forces were exhausted. The British plan now changed, from one of establishing a forward defensive line at Romani to one of re-occupying the entire Sinai Desert and establishing its advanced line nearer the Egypt–Palestine border at El Arish. The EEF began a more steady advance, relatively slow but methodical as its logistics were built up behind it. Each Ottoman garrison was attacked and captured in turn, although generally the main Ottoman forces managed to slip away before being completely overwhelmed. This led to a conviction among the EEF's senior commanders (and utterly at odds with their recent experiences in the Dardanelles) that the Ottomans were poor troops who would not stand and fight. When the last two garrisons in the desert, at Magdhaba and El Magruntein (Rafa), were attacked in December 1916 and January 1917, the mounted forces deliberately encircled them first to prevent their escape, tactics that very nearly led to failure in both cases. This strange assessment of Ottoman fighting ability would lead to disaster at Gaza the following year.

THE CAMPAIGN

BUILDING THEIR LOGISTICS

At the start of 1916, the British and Ottoman Empires faced each other across the Sinai Desert. This 190km (120-mile) wide expanse of intrinsically worthless but strategically vital terrain separated British Egypt from Ottoman Palestine, and control of the desert would effectively lead to control of the Suez Canal. The desert was a formidable obstacle. Along the northern edge was a corridor around 30–40km (20–25 miles) deep where the sands were relatively flat, with large areas of shifting dunes, and prone to thick morning mists rolling in off the Mediterranean. To the south, for the next 100km (60 miles), rocky hills soon began to rise, steadily turning into mountains by the time they reach the line roughly between Suez and Aqaba. From there south into the rest of the Sinai Peninsula, inhospitable mountains prevailed. There were three primary routes across the Sinai: the northern route near the coast, the central through the foothills to the south, and the southern through the mountains. This latter route was impassable to wheeled transport, while the central could only take wagons or artillery with considerable effort. Although smaller forces and camel patrols would operate in the central and southern regions, in effect any military operations would be limited to the northern, coastal strip, and even then only after the development of significant logistical infrastructure.

This strip included the basin around Qatia, in the west, where low-lying ground led to a proliferation of oases and wells, but further east the land gradually rose, and the water became more brackish and harder to find. The water here was often suitable only for the use of horses and camels, and even then only barely. Areas where water was available in quantity, such as the small settlements at El Arish, Bir el Mazar and in the Qatia basin, formed natural strategic focal points. Even with these waypoints, traversing the desert in any strength and then maintaining the forces deployed presented serious logistical challenges, and ones that stretched far beyond the borders of the desert itself. Both the British and Ottoman forces were operating at the end of tenuous lines

Adequate supplies of water were the main limiting factor for both sides in determining the size and disposition of forces in the Sinai. This Ottoman pumping station was at El Arish. (Library of Congress Prints and Photographs Division)

of communications. The British might have been well established in Egypt, but most military resources had to be shipped to the country from the UK, India, New Zealand, Australia or from across the Atlantic. Once in Egypt, these resources had to be shared across not just the Canal defences but also the forces in the Western Desert, Salonika, Aden and other areas around the eastern Mediterranean. While the end of the Gallipoli campaign across December 1915 and early January 1916 led to a great influx of troops, this created its own organizational problems and continued to strain the army's logistics. Command structures were confused, with multiple headquarters and staffs overseeing troops in the same areas. Only in March 1916, with the creation of a dedicated EEF and the steady withdrawal of the former MEF troops to France, did the situation begin to clarify. Even then, the EEF's commander, Sir Archibald Murray, had broad responsibility for the political and military governance of Egypt and logistical support for British forces around the Eastern Mediterranean, all of which diverted attention and materiel from the Sinai.

For the Ottomans, whose empire was (unlike Britain's) mostly a solid mass, the situation should have been easier. They were on their own borders and had the benefit of interior lines of communication, but those lines were deeply flawed. A single main railway ran from Constantinople into the southern

Both sides would lay hundreds of miles of pipelines across the desert. Here, German officers supervise the laying of smaller branch pipes in the eastern Sinai.

Camels remained crucial to both sides and were always in short supply. Egypt was a net importer of camels before 1914, and the war cut off its main supply from Arabia.

portions of the empire, but there were gaps in the line in the mountains of Anatolia, and the network across Greater Syria was skeletal. This province, covering essentially the areas from Aleppo south to the Sinai, east across the Jordan Valley and south into Arabia, lacked any significant industry and had few centres of population. Although the railway ran to Damascus, from there the main line crossed the Jordan and ran down into the Arabian Peninsula – the famous Hedjaz Railway. A branch line ran down to Jaffa and Jerusalem, but at the start of the war, these lines stopped well short of the frontier. The Ottoman Governor of Greater Syria and commander of the 4th Army that garrisoned it, Djemal Pasha, put enormous effort into extending the railways from 1915. He ran a line to Beersheba, the administrative centre for the Negev region, and from there into the eastern portions of the Sinai Desert. However, rails were in high demand across the empire, and wood suitable for use as sleepers was extremely rare across Palestine and Syria. Once the trains began running over the extended network, shortages of coal meant that local wood became even more scarce as it was used as fuel.

Military supplies and troops also had to be fought for against the demands of other fronts. Although the end of the Gallipoli campaign in early 1916 would free up significant numbers of troops for use elsewhere, the campaigns in the Caucasus, the Balkans, Mesopotamia and (from the summer of 1916) Arabia all vied for these resources. Troops recruited in Syria and Palestine were just as likely to be sent to other regions, while the food and other supplies harvested there were also liable to be sent elsewhere. The plagues of locusts that repeatedly swept through the region in 1915 had already led to severe food shortages, and stockpiling supplies for future military campaigns was extremely problematic.

In December 1915, the 1st Expeditionary Corps was formed under the command of the German Colonel Friedrich Freiherr Kress von Kressenstein. Previously, Kressenstein had been Djemal's Chief of Staff during the first attack on the Suez Canal, and had later been left in command of the Desert

The British developed a huge base depot at Kantara, from where their main railway ran into the desert.

Command, harassing the Canal defences. He had been heavily involved in building up the logistics and lines of communications in Palestine and the eastern fringes of the Sinai, and he now began to receive forces with which to re-occupy the desert. Efforts were not confined to the northern route, with the wells and water cisterns at Jifjafa, around 80km (50 miles) from the Canal on the central route, also seeing significant development from December 1915. However, most of the efforts were concentrated on the coastal strip, and troops continued to develop the base at El Arish, where a hospital was established and, in April 1916, an airfield to support aircraft from FA300, which had its main base at Beersheba. Equipped with six Rumpler C.1 two seaters and two Pfalz E.II monoplane fighters, FA300 was outnumbered by Nos 14 and 17 Squadrons of the RFC in Egypt, each of which was larger than the single FA, but the German aircraft easily outclassed the British Royal Aircraft Factory BE2s. Becoming operational in mid-April, the German aircraft made several bombing raids on the British Canal defences and even Port Said in short order, doing little physical damage but having a disproportionate effect on military and civilian morale, while also providing Kressenstein with invaluable intelligence on British positions.

However, the build up was too slow for the central Ottoman authorities, who were coming under pressure from their German allies to strike as soon as possible. Some 11 British, Australian or New Zealand infantry divisions had been withdrawn from Gallipoli to Egypt, and another three were being formed from the large ANZAC depots in the country, while two divisions of Indian infantry had been defending the Canal since 1914. Already some of these

The British railway generally lagged far behind the advance troops, but was still vital for moving water and other supplies out towards the front lines.

The Royal Flying Corps' aircraft, like this BE2c, were important for gathering intelligence over wide areas, but were far from infallible. Troops and camps often showed up poorly against the bland desert.

divisions were being sent to France, where the main British Expeditionary Force was preparing for its summer offensive on the Somme, and it was clear that others would follow. The Germans wanted to keep pressure on the British in Egypt to ensure that these divisions remained on defensive duties in the desert, and so in early April, Kressenstein began his advance from El Arish. His column consisted of some 3,700 men, including the 1st, 2nd and parts of the 3rd Battalions of the 32nd Regiment, a thousand irregular Arabs of the Hedjaz Camel Regiment, six artillery pieces and four machine guns.

In truth, the main strategic purpose of Kressenstein's expedition was already out of date. Even before he had set out, six of the infantry divisions in Egypt had been sent to France and a seventh to Mesopotamia. Three more would go to France (along with the Indian divisions) by the end of June.

The Casualty Clearing Station set up for the anticipated casualties from the Jifjafa Raid, 11–14 April 1916. Wheeled ambulances, sand carts or 'cacolets' (stretchers slung one either side of a camel) would carry the wounded back to field hospitals.

In all, 232,000 British troops were withdrawn from Egypt in the first six months of 1916, leaving four infantry divisions (the 42nd (East Lancashire), 52nd (Lowland), 53rd (Welsh) and 54th (East Anglian) Divisions), a handful of cavalry brigades and several battalions of the Imperial Camel Corps to form the EEF. At an operational level though, his objective was still valid; if he could establish an advanced base of operations closer to the Canal, he could still disrupt the shipping flowing through it as well as preparing the site for a much larger body of troops to arrive over the summer.

AFFAIR AT QATIA

The EEF was also starting its advance into the Sinai. The main defensive lines remained along the Suez Canal, which was broken into three numbered sections running from south to north, each garrisoned by a changing and dwindling number of divisions and brigades as forces were withdrawn for redeployment. The main railway line was pushing east from the EEF's base depot at Kantara, while a second, narrow-gauge line was being built along the coast east from Port Said. These were in the northern No. 3 Canal Section, under the command of General the Hon. Herbert Lawrence. The initial objective for the main line was Dueidar, about 23km (14 miles) east of Kantara, from where it would run north-east towards Romani, about another 16km (10 miles) further on. An infantry outpost was established at Dueidar, where trenches were dug and a thin layer of barbed wire (more for warning purposes than a serious obstacle) was laid out. Meanwhile, the 5th Mounted Brigade (Queen's Own Worcestershire Hussars (QOWH), Royal Gloucestershire Hussars (RGH) and the Warwickshire Yeomanry) under Brigadier-General Edgar Wiggin was sent to the Romani area. Tasked with escorting parties from the 413th Field Squadron, Royal Engineers, who would be developing wells at Romani and, to the east and south-east, at Qatia and Hamisah, the 5th Mounted Brigade was spread out in smaller detachments across a broad area. Their standing orders were to withdraw should they encounter any serious Ottoman opposition, as any reinforcements from the Canal zone would take at least two days to arrive.

A series of tented camps were set up, although the defence of these sites does not seem to have been a major consideration. These troops were veterans of the Gallipoli campaign, and it may be that the wide open areas seemingly far from any front line engendered a false sense of security, or their standing orders may have suggested that none were needed, as they would simply withdraw if attacked. It could also have been that they lacked the resources to establish proper entrenchments. Some small trenches were dug, but in the soft sand of the Sinai, decent-sized trenches needed a wooden framework and revetment to maintain their shape for any length of time. Either way, although regular patrols began

A patrol from the Queen's Own Worcestershire Hussars (QOWH) rest while on patrol. Horses would be frequently rested to prevent saddle sores and other health issues. (Trustees of the Queen's Own Worcestershire Hussars Museum)

to sweep the desert and encounter hostile Ottoman patrols, none of the isolated 5th Mounted Brigade units took more than rudimentary steps to secure their camps.

The skirmishing of patrols led to a small but steady stream of casualties, and on 9 April four troops of the QOWH were despatched to attack an Ottoman camp at Bir el Abd, about 24km (15 miles) east. A force of around 100 Ottomans were pushed out of the camp and a running fight ensued, although after a few hours of operating in the soft sand the Yeomen's horses became exhausted and a withdrawal was ordered. On 19 April, a Warwickshire Yeomanry patrol was attacked and pinned down to a hilltop, and the QOWH had to send a squadron to relieve them. Two days later, the relieving squadron (D Squadron) was despatched from Qatia to Oghratina, about 8km (5 miles) east, where water sources had already been scouted. With them went 40–50 engineers to develop the wells, and the following day A Squadron QOWH joined them. The unit commander, Major Frank Williams-Thomas, established a rough camp on a hilltop just south of the road, and ordered slit trenches dug in around the edges.

That same day, 22 April, Brigadier-General Wiggin received a reconnaissance report from the RFC to say that a force of 200–300 Ottoman troops was encamped at Mageibra, about 13km (8 miles) south-east of his post at Hamisah. His forces were more thinly spread than ever by then, but he estimated that he could lead a large force on a night march to attack Mageibra at dawn, returning his troops to their posts by the middle of the day. He sent his plan to General Lawrence and asked for permission to attack; this, he felt, would help push back the Ottoman forces in the area and reduce the friction his patrols were experiencing. After requesting various clarifications, and knowing that a force of Australian Light Horse (ALH) were already en route to reinforce Wiggin, Lawrence approved.

Men of C Squadron QOWH pose with local Arabs, Qatia, late March 1916. Within a month, all but three of these Yeomen were dead or prisoners. (Trustees of the Queen's Own Worcestershire Hussars Museum)

The camp at Qatia, days before the attack. (Trustees of the Queen's Own Worcestershire Hussars Museum)

Wiggin gathered his forces at Hamisah. Two squadrons of the Warwicks (B and D) and C Squadron of the QOWH, with their regimental commander, Lieutenant Colonel the Hon. Charles Coventry, gathered and set off into the desert after midnight into a thick mist. This left two squadrons of RGH at Romani, A Squadron of the RGH at Qatia, and A and D Squadrons of the QOWH at Oghratina, each accompanied by detachments of Royal Engineers, Army Service Corps, Army Ordnance Corps and Army Veterinary Corps troops.

When Wiggin arrived at Mageibra at dawn, the camp was all but empty. The force there, much larger than estimated, was the Left Column of Kressenstein's expedition and had left the previous night to attack Dueidar. There, Captain Frederick Roberts had his own company of the 1/5th Battalion Royal Scots Fusiliers (RSF) plus small detachments from the Bikaner Camel Corps and the Queen's Own Royal Glasgow Yeomanry, 256 men in all. Also enveloped in thick mist, the piquets at Dueidar were alerted by noise from their wire before dawn and a sporadic fight developed along their front, becoming more intense as the dawn burned off the mist. At 0700hrs, a relief column of two companies of the 1/4th RSF and a few Yeomen left Hill 70, taking two hours to traverse the 11km (7 miles) to Dueidar. Roberts' men had held out, and with the arrival of reinforcements were able to counter-attack, later being supported by the rest of the 1/4th RSF and the 5th Regiment ALH. Dueidar had been held.

For the 5th Mounted Brigade, the day would not end so well. What followed on Easter Sunday, 23 April 1916, was a fight complicated by distances, poor communications and, in the early morning at least, a thick mist. It would demonstrate many of the issues that would be continuing problems throughout the rest of the campaign.

A large Ottoman force proceeded down the road just to the north of the hill at Oghratina held by the QOWH. Ottoman cameliers stopped to water

Arab irregular cameliers leave Beersheba, 1916.

their animals at the foot of the hill, seemingly unaware of the British troops above them. An aircraft from FA300 had reconnoitred this area on 20 April, before the move to Oghratina and a slight shift in the location of the Qatia camp, and it would become clear that Kressenstein's force was relying heavily on this information.

With an enemy force of unknown size just to his north, and possibly on other sides too, Williams-Thomas faced a decision. His standing orders said he should retreat, and his mounted men might be able to slip south into the desert. However, that would leave around 50 dismounted men moving more slowly behind who would be vulnerable to being overrun by the Ottoman mounted troops, and as yet it seemed that the enemy had not detected them. He decided to remain in place, and reported his situation via telegraph to Qatia. Shortly before 0500hrs, the Ottomans discovered his presence and began to surround the hill, attacking from the south-west. For 90 minutes, the advancing Ottoman troops were held at bay, until the sole British machine gun was knocked out. As casualties mounted, Williams-Thomas was forced to shorten his line, pulling back from the edge of the hilltop and allowing the attackers to gain a foothold. By 0800hrs, only 65 of his 200 Yeoman were still unwounded, and only half of them had working rifles. With the fog now lifting to show Kressenstein's main force marching towards them, Williams-Thomas ordered his men to surrender.

To his west at Qatia, Captain Lloyd-Baker's force was only half his size. Alerted by telegraph and the sound of firing, Lloyd-Baker was also hampered by the mist and a large number of dismounted troops, while reports from Dueidar implied that there may be large enemy forces to his west as well as the east. He, too, decided to delay implementing his standing orders and stay in place to await developments. While perhaps laudable, or at least understandable, like Williams-Thomas before him, he would be losing his main advantage in the face of superior numbers – mobility.

Ottoman irregulars in action at Qatia. Note the single-shot Peabody-Martini carbines, purchased by the Ottomans in the 1870s and still used due to wartime shortages of equipment.

At approximately 0930hrs, Ottoman artillery began falling a short distance from his positions, at the location where the remains of the QOWH camp stood. This continued until 1000hrs, when a German aircraft appeared and, realizing that the QOWH camp was largely empty, redirected their fire onto the RGH positions. The first shells landed on the horse lines, inflicting tremendous casualties among the animals and further limiting Lloyd-Baker's options.

The artillery fire ceased at 1030hrs, as British troops appeared to the north. This was the rest of the RGH, under Lieutenant Colonel Ralph Yorke, who had left Romani as soon as the mist had cleared. Their sudden appearance forced the artillery to relocate, but a screen of Ottoman infantry deployed and the relieving troops were forced to dismount and fight. At around the same time, C Squadron of the QOWH, under Colonel Coventry, also appeared from the south. Wiggin had ordered his men back to Hamisah where he received reports of the fighting at Oghratina. However, his force needed to water their horses before undertaking any further marches. Coventry had asked to water his horses first so he could ride to rejoin his regiment, but by the time he was leading his squadron north it was clear that the fight at Oghratina was over. Instead, he led his men to Qatia, moving around behind the camp to take up position just to the north of Lloyd-Baker's line, although he was unable to make contact with either RGH formation. An hour later, General Wiggin led his two Warwick squadrons into the fight, but just as with Colonel Yorke, they encountered stiff resistance, this time from Arab cameliers, and were also forced to dismount, losing their manoeuvrability.

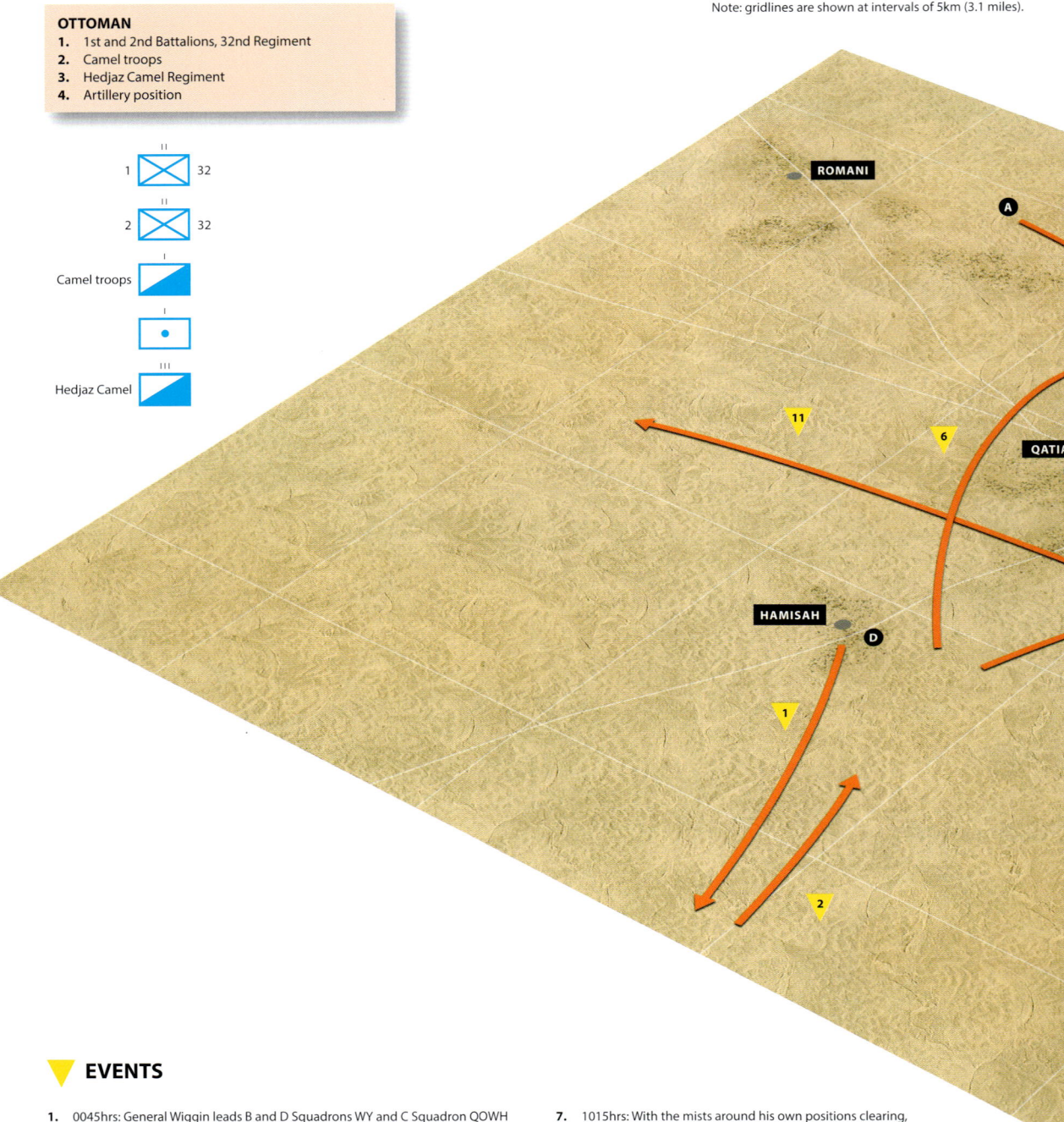

OTTOMAN
1. 1st and 2nd Battalions, 32nd Regiment
2. Camel troops
3. Hedjaz Camel Regiment
4. Artillery position

Note: gridlines are shown at intervals of 5km (3.1 miles).

EVENTS

1. 0045hrs: General Wiggin leads B and D Squadrons WY and C Squadron QOWH (with Colonel Coventry) south from Hamisah to ride to Mageibra.

2. 0415hrs: Wiggin's force reaches Mageibra to find the camp empty. They rest for two hours before returning to Hamisah.

3. 0430hrs: Piquets from A and D Squadrons QOWH report movements in the morning mist. Soon, hostile cameliers are spotted.

4. 0445hrs: Ottoman forces begin to envelope and attack the Yeomen at Oghratina. The fighting continues until 0745hrs.

5. 0930hrs: A Squadron RGH at Qatia comes under shellfire from an unseen Ottoman force. Infantry attacks soon follow.

6. 1015hrs: Colonel Coventry and C Squadron QOWH, having watered their horses at Hamisah, ride around behind A Squadron RGH and take up positions to their north, just out of touch.

7. 1015hrs: With the mists around his own positions clearing, Colonel Yorke leads most of B and D Squadrons RGH from Romani towards Qatia.

8. 1030hrs: The Ottoman artillery ceases as Colonel Yorke's force nears, forcing them to relocate to the south. Yorke deploys his men, but at 1300hrs is forced to halt due to casualties.

9. 1130hrs: General Wiggin leads B and D Squadrons WY up from the south, although he too is forced to go to ground at 1345hrs.

10. 1445hrs: The Ottomans stage a final attack, and at 1500hrs the British line breaks. Qatia is overrun.

11. 1500hrs: Seeing Qatia fall, General Wiggin orders his force back to Hamisah, and from there to Dueidar, arriving at 2100hrs.

12. 1500hrs: Colonel Yorke also orders a retreat to Romani, and from there with his whole force back to the railhead, arriving at 0300hrs on 24 April.

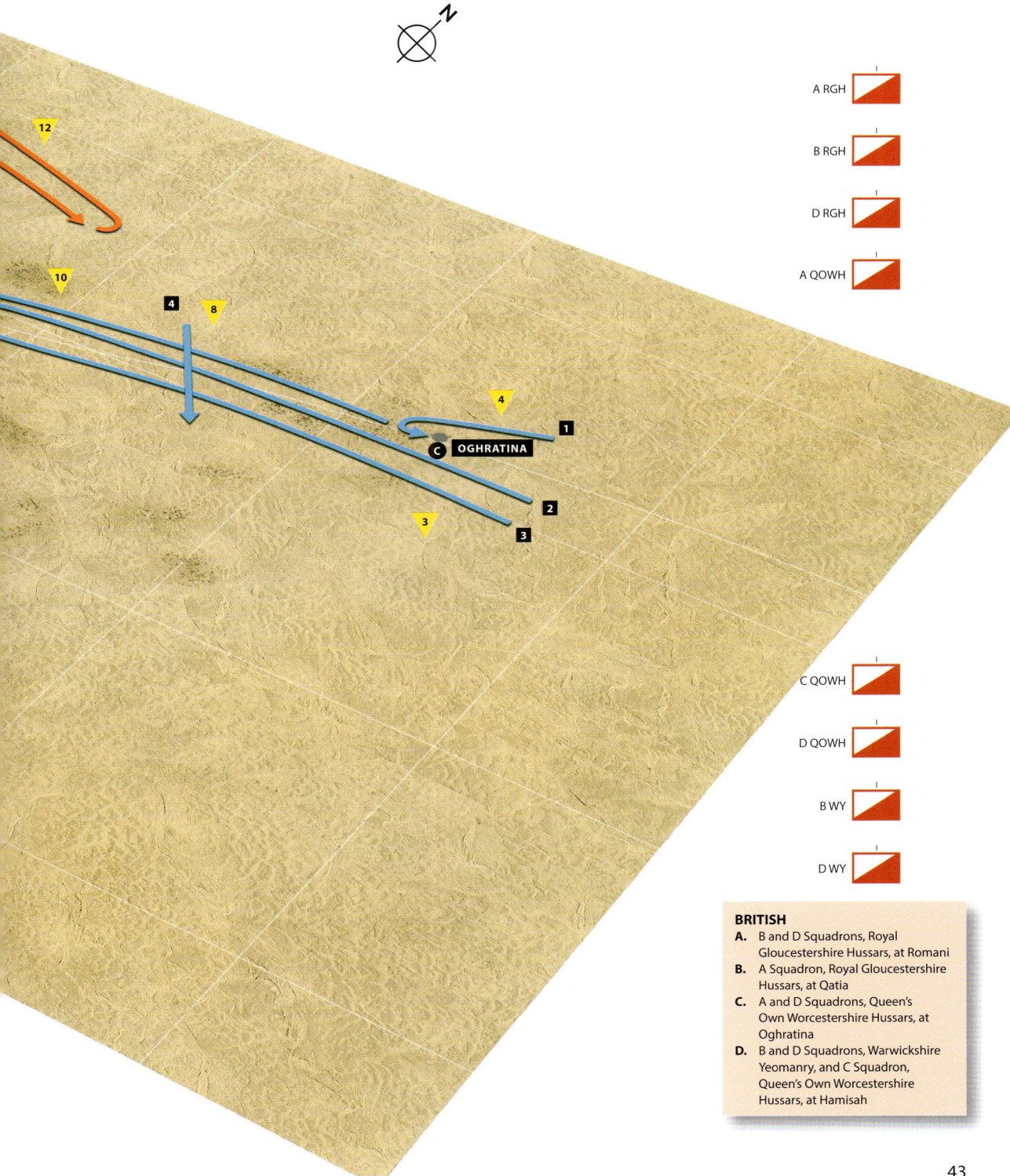

DECISION AT QATIA, 1330HRS, 23 APRIL 1916 (PP. 44–45)

At 1330hrs, Colonel Charles Coventry **(1)** (commanding the QOWH) called for Captain William 'Bill' Wiggin **(2)** (commanding C Squadron QOWH) and ordered him to go back to the horse-holders. Accounts differ as to why: Wiggin would say he was ordered to bring up the one-in-four men holding the horses to reinforce the line; Coventry would say it was to order him to ride to General E. A. Wiggin and guide him to their position **(3)**; others say it was to bring forward the horses so the squadron could retreat. Captain Wiggin was wounded by shrapnel and fell unconscious before he could complete his task, so it is a moot point, but it demonstrated that Coventry had realised his position was untenable and made the decision to change the situation. Like his fellow commanders, he was outnumbered, out of touch with the other Yeomanry forces **(4)** and in a poor tactical situation. With only their basic webbing, his men were running low on both water and ammunition **(5)**, and while their pith helmets gave some protection from the sun, they were awkward and gave no protection from enemy fire **(6)**. A number of Yeomen had also had their rifles jam in the soft sand **(7)**.

By dismounting to fight on foot, the Yeomanry had lost the advantage of mobility. Once dismounted, they were easily pinned in place and out-gunned by the Ottomans. Captain Wiggin later regained consciousness to find the RGH squadrons on their right flank had collapsed, and his own squadron was in disarray. He managed to gather and lead the survivors of his regiment – 54 NCOs and men – to safety. Wiggin was awarded the Distinguished Service Order for his actions that day, and later received a second one for leading his regiment's troops in the charge at Huj in 1917.

Around 600 Yeomen were now in action against an Ottoman force three or four times their size and supported by artillery. The sun was nearing its zenith, and for the troops lining the sand dunes there was no shelter and little chance to refill their water bottles. They were only able to support each other in the broadest terms, and with all of them forced to fight on foot they had lost their main advantage. It was now the middle of the day, and the troops were fighting while laying on hot sand under a blazing sun, while increasing numbers of weapons were becoming jammed with the fine sand (a phenomenon widely reported during this action, although there are few references to it in other skirmishes).

The Bikaner Camel Corps was raised by Maharaja Ganga Singh of Bikaner, and served on the Canal defences from the early months of the war.

At 1300hrs, with an increasing number of casualties and a fear of being surrounded, Yorke began a steady retreat towards Romani. An hour later, Wiggin, to the south, found he could make no further progress towards his trapped men, and finally at 1500hrs, the lines around Qatia broke. It appears that the surviving commander (Lloyd-Baker had been killed early on) of the RGH ordered his men to break out to the west. With their flank wide open, Coventry ordered his men to stand and receive the final Ottoman attack, before quickly ordering them to surrender instead. Some QOWH Yeomen did attempt to break out, and about half the squadron managed to escape. Some 17 men of A Squadron RGH escaped.

Wiggin, seeing the defence collapse and worried about his own flanks and rear, now ordered a retreat to Hamisah and then Dueidar. His brigade had suffered severely. One squadron of the RGH, about 100 men, had been lost, while around 350 Worcester Yeomen had been killed or captured, with only one officer and 54 men able to parade the next day. The RGH and QOWH were formed into a Composite Regiment for the next six months.

Kressenstein was now in control of the Qatia area, although British outposts remained to his north-west near Romani and south-west at Dueidar. He had met with unexpected resistance and had experienced poor communications and coordination among his own forces during the resulting fight. He had taken around 10 per cent casualties, and was receiving reports that British reinforcements were already on their way. Kressenstein decided that his position was untenable. The following day, he fell back towards Bir el Mazar, with the RFC harassing his columns and the ALH re-occupying Qatia and then Oghratina behind him, rescuing several wounded Yeomen and burying the dead. At the end of the month, Kressenstein was back in Beersheba, having lost 10 per cent of his force and failing to establish a forward post. The EEF also abandoned the immediate Qatia area, and fell back to establish a new forward defensive line at Romani.

DIGGING IN AT ROMANI

As further British troops moved into the Romani area, and also expanded the depth and width of the defences between Romani and the Canal, work continued to improve the logistics to support the forward troops. In January, recruitment had started for an Egyptian Labour Corps (ELC), to provide workers for the expansion of the road and rail network, load and off load material at Kantara and other supply depots, and to man the Camel Transport Corps (CTC). While the railway, which had reached around 8km (5 miles) west of Romani at the end of April and Romani itself on 15 May, moved the bulk of supplies into the desert, camels were still needed to move them from the railway to the forward troops and outposts. Once it reached Romani, construction was paused until July, and the personnel and material were diverted into creating branch lines in the rear areas. Construction of the mainline started again on 7 July, pushing 6km (4 miles) in 11 days before again pausing, presumably to avoid the anticipated battle.

In July 1916, work also began on a water pipeline, running from the extensive system of cisterns and pipelines that had been developed in the Canal zone over the previous year. This began to pump water from the Sweet Water Canal through a complex series of filtration systems to remove debris, wildlife and parasites, and into massive cisterns along the Canal. This process alone needed some 240km (150 miles) of pipes, and used most of the stocks available in Egypt. Although work began on the pumps, cisterns and other infrastructure needed to operate the pipeline into the desert, it was not until the arrival in September of another 210km (130 miles) of 12in piping from India that proper progress could start on the line towards Romani. It paralleled the railway, where further cisterns were built at regular

Men of the Highland Light Infantry lay the 'wire road'. Strictly for infantry use (no animals or wheeled transport were allowed), this consisted of overlapping strips of wire mesh which provided firm footing in the soft sand, allowing the men to march faster and farther.

intervals, and much of the water was needed to keep the engines running and providing for the camels and troops on the lines of communications.

For troops at or near the front lines, the often saline water pulled from the desert wells (and usually made worse by the medical officers adding chlorine tablets to 'clean' the water) were still the staple. Soldiers were rationed one gallon per man per day; five pints of this went to the cookhouse, two were for drinking, and one was for hygiene. This ration was not always met, and hygiene was generally the first thing to fall by the wayside. Stomach complaints and sores were prevalent, caused by the abrasive sand as well as the lack of washing facilities. Drinking water was usually only issued before dawn and after dark, so that it would not be immediately sweated back out. Gunner Anthony Bluett recalled the problems of adjusting to working in the desert:

> There followed days of unremitting toil… With bowed backs and blistered hands [we] shovelled up half the desert and put it down somewhere else; the other half we put into sandbags and made gun pits of them. We dug places for the artificers, kitchens for the cooks, walled-in places for forage, and but for the timely arrival of a battalion of Indian infantry we should have dug the trenches round the camp; we were mercifully spared that, however. By way of change we dug holes: big holes, little holes, round holes, square holes, rectangular holes; holes for refuse, wide, deep holes for washing-pits; every kind of hole you can think of and many you can't. Day by day the sun waxed stronger until work became a torture unspeakable and hardly to be borne. With the slightest exertion the perspiration ran in rivulets from face and finger-tips; clothes became saturated and clung like a glove to our dripping bodies; and if a man stood for a time in one place the sand around was sodden with his sweat.

In the early summer, the EEF had to adapt to a growing air threat, as is shown with these camouflaged infantry tents.

Conditions were harsh. Troops and animals suffered from the heat, sand, flies and lack of water. Food varied in quality. Near the railhead, fresh vegetables and fresh or frozen meat were readily available, but troops operating further afield would mostly subsist on dried fruit, tins of bully beef (which turned into saline mush in the heat), tins of stew and army biscuits, which were almost inedible in the dry heat. Animals were provided fodder, but had to be fed carefully to avoid ingesting sand. It took some months for the British forces to acclimatize. Although the Australians were more used to a hot and dry climate, many were from urban areas and unused to living rough for extended periods. Across the whole EEF, sickness rates were generally high, and few units were ever close to full strength. The health of animals and men was always a major concern for field commanders.

For all that forward movement had ceased, the British stance was far from passive or defensive. Two weeks before the affair at Qatia, a small force of Light Horsemen and cameliers had attacked and destroyed the Ottoman cisterns at Jifjafa, seriously inhibiting the Ottomans' already tenuous ability to use the central route across the Sinai. In May and June, raids were made on the wells and cisterns at Bir Salama, Wadi um Mukhsheid and Moiya Harab, and the RFC and AFC launched a large-scale bombing raid against the German airfield at El Arish. Patrols were constantly scouring the desert, and on 16 May, patrols of Light Horsemen and Mounted Riflemen were caught by the Khamsin, an oven-like hot wind that blows from across the Sahara, near Bir Bayud, experiencing temperatures of over 50°C (120°F). Many men and horses required evacuation and medical attention, requiring several weeks to recuperate.

Anti-aircraft guns also had to be improvised, such as with this Vickers heavy machine gun on a makeshift mount. Few weapons could easily be aimed at the high angles needed without adaptation.

The EEF's high command was still receiving intelligence that large Ottoman forces were gathering in Palestine. Some of the wilder estimates ran to 250,000 or more troops being prepared to make the next attack, although Murray and his staff considered 100,000 to be optimistic and an upper estimate. Such a force would pose a serious threat, and so work was begun to construct a line of redoubts on high ground east of Romani. Beginning on the coast (and, confusingly, numbered in construction order rather than linear placement) a total of 17 redoubts were built, ranging from Post 11 on the coast down in a line passing just to the east of Romani to Katib Gannit, a prominent sand dune approximately 30m (100ft) high to the south-east of Romani. This formed a natural southern-flank mark for the positions, and Post 2 stood at the southern edge, while Posts 1, 21, 21A, 22, 22A and 23 formed a line running back to the north-west, along the edge of Wellington Ridge, to protect the open flank. The north–south line was about 8km (5 miles) long, while 6.5km

(4 miles) west of Wellington Ridge was another prominent height, dubbed Mount Royston. Some 5km (3 miles) north-west of Mount Royston stood the smaller Canterbury Hill, with Pelusium Station on the railway near behind.

The line of redoubts was garrisoned by the 52nd (Lowland) Division under the temporary command of General W. E. B. Smith, with the 158th Brigade attached from the 53rd (Welsh) Division. With an average spacing of 700m (750yds) between redoubts, each was held by 40–170 men (the average was 100), 1–3 heavy machine guns and whatever Lewis guns the garrison troops had. The southern redoubts, where the ground was quite broken, also had Stokes trench mortars. Barbed wire was sparsely laid by Western Front standards, but thick enough to delay and deflect Ottoman troops. The 52nd Division was at around two-thirds strength, and had about one-third of its actual strength in the redoubts. The other troops were spaced in reserve at intervals along the rear of the line; with the soft sand of the area, moving quickly over long distances would be difficult.

This view, taken after the battle, shows the open slopes and sparse barbed wire in front of the redoubt line at Romani.

The division's artillery was also understrength, with just 36 guns along the whole line. One battery of large 60-pdrs and two batteries of 18-pdrs were positioned close to the railway. Another battery of 18-pdrs covered the northern end of the line, while one 18-pdr battery and two 4.5in howitzer batteries were positioned in the 'hook' of the redoubts to the south.

Behind the southern flank of the British line, west of the 'hook' and north of Wellington Ridge, was the camp of the 1st and 2nd Brigades of the A&NZ Mounted Division under General Harry Chauvel, consisting of five regiments of Australian Light Horse and the Wellington Regiment of the New Zealand Mounted Rifles. (The 3rd Light Horse Brigade remained back in the Canal defences.) Further to the rear, the New Zealand Mounted Rifles Brigade (with the 5th Regiment Australian Light Horse attached) and remains of the 5th Mounted Brigade garrisoned the area between Hill 70 and Pelusium Station. All of these troops came under the No. 3 Canal Section and under the umbrella command of General Lawrence.

In late July, Murray and his senior commanders drew up a plan to receive the Ottoman attack that intelligence reports assured them was coming. With some 14,000 men of the EEF in place at Romani, they were facing a confused picture of what they could expect to be sent against them. The wild estimates provided by some intelligence sources have already been noted, and in fact, the expeditionary force being gathered by Kressenstein would number just 16,000 men.

A file of Light Horsemen ready for patrol.

It was decided by the British to take a defensive posture for the time being. It was estimated that the Ottomans would not be able to attack Romani before 3 or 4 August. By that date, elements of the 42nd (East Lancashire) Division should have been arriving at Romani, and if no Ottoman attack had developed by 13 August, then a cautious advance would be made. Each day, one of the A&NZ Mounted Division brigades was sent east to make contact with, harass and scout the Ottoman's outposts and advancing troops. The second brigade would spend a day 'resting', deployed to the south of Katib Gannit, extending the British line by another 6.5km (4 miles). It was fully expected that the enemy would attempt to swing around this open desert flank to cut off the British troops at Romani and attack them from the rear. The ANZAC piquet line, which was not allowed to prepare any defensive positions that might be spotted by the enemy (although telephone lines were laid), was intended to detect and disrupt that attack, breaking it up before slowly swinging back with their left flank hinged on Katib Gannit, until running on an east–west line out along Wellington Ridge to Mount Royston. Once the Ottoman attack had been sucked into this area, infantry and mounted forces at Pelusium Station and Hill 70 would attack their open flank and roll them back into the desert.

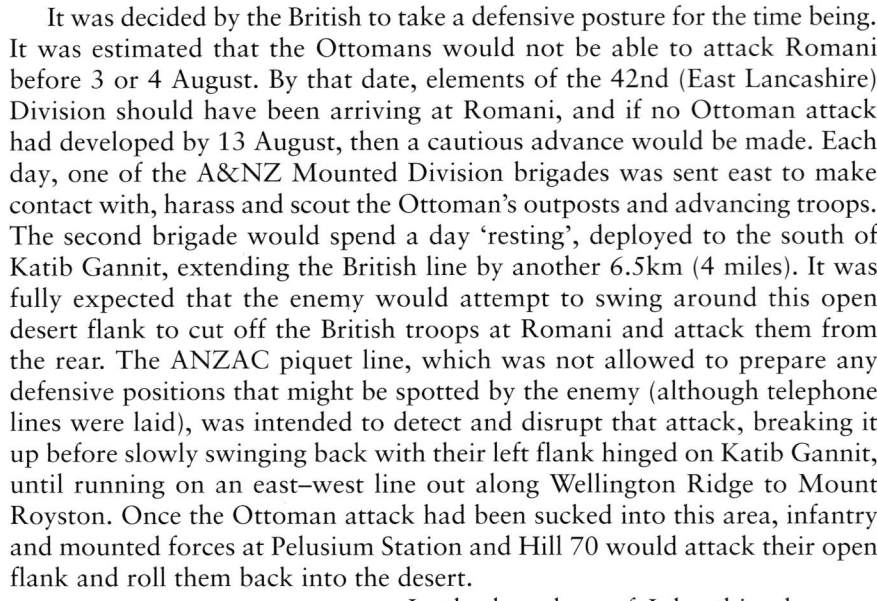

New Zealand Mounted Riflemen being trained on a Lewis light machine gun before the Battle of Romani. In 1917, light machine guns would be standardized with Lewis guns for the infantry and cameliers, and Hotchkiss Mk. 1 guns for the cavalry. (Auckland War Memorial Museum Tāmaki Paenga Hira, PH-ALB-210-p12-2)

In the last days of July, this plan was finalized, agreed and approved by Murray, who also suggested that Lawrence move his headquarters forward from the Canal to the Romani area in order to have better command of his forces. Lawrence declined, in a decision that has been frequently criticized since. Although no reason was given, it is known that the British high command (including Murray) was concerned that further, undetected, Ottoman forces were lurking to the south of the main thrust. Both aerial and traditional reconnaissance methods had proved of limited use in the desert, and it had been noted that no Ottoman cavalry had so far been seen. A large force, including cavalry, could be aiming to make a sudden, deeper flanking move around the Romani position. Although a mobile column of mounted troops (a mix of Imperial Camel Corps, Yeomanry and Light Horse) was formed in No. 2 Section to cover part of the gap, it clearly still played on the British commanders' minds. Lawrence may have wanted to stay back to watch and communicate better with the broader front rather than being focused too much on Romani. As it was, he would have limited control over the battle when it came, especially when the main telephone lines were cut by enemy artillery fire.

The Battle of Romani, 4 August 1916

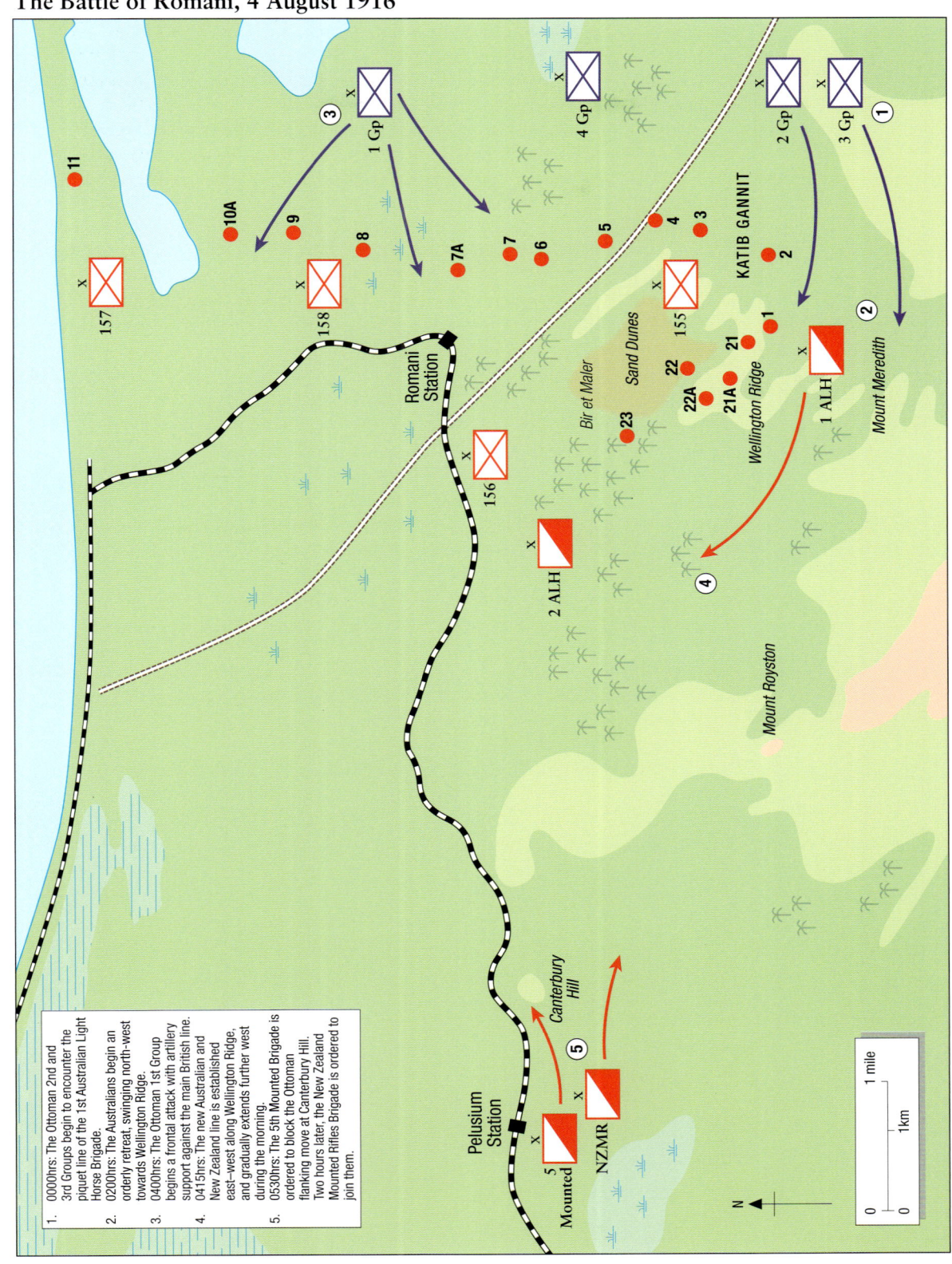

1. 0000hrs: The Ottoman 2nd and 3rd Groups begin to encounter the piquet line of the 1st Australian Light Horse Brigade.
2. 0200hrs: The Australians begin an orderly retreat, swinging north-west towards Wellington Ridge.
3. 0400hrs: The Ottoman 1st Group begins a frontal attack with artillery support against the main British line.
4. 0415hrs: The new Australian and New Zealand line is established east–west along Wellington Ridge, and gradually extends further west during the morning.
5. 0530hrs: The 5th Mounted Brigade is ordered to block the Ottoman flanking move at Canterbury Hill. Two hours later, the New Zealand Mounted Rifles Brigade is ordered to join them.

BATTLE OF ROMANI

On 28 July, Kressenstein had begun his final advance. For some weeks, he had been moving troops in smaller columns into the desert from El Arish via Bir el Mazar to the Qatia and Oghratina area. Closing on the British positions and receiving the latest intelligence from his own scouts and the German air contingent, Kressenstein drew up his final plans. Despite opposition from some of his senior Ottoman staff, who viewed the British positions as too strong, he decided to attack. His 1st Expeditionary Force was based around the Ottoman 3rd Infantry Division, consisting of the 31st, 32nd and 39th Regiments (each with four battalions) and supporting Ottoman, Austro-Hungarian and German heavy weapons. Kressenstein split this into four Groups: 1st Group (31st Regiment, two German machine-gun companies, a battery of mountain guns and three batteries of heavy artillery) under Colonel Refet would attack the line of redoubts head on; 2nd and 3rd Groups (each with three battalions of the other two regiments, two German machine-gun companies and a battery of mountain guns) under Colonel Ibrahim and Major Muhlman would attack around the southern flank and sweep into the British rear; while the 4th Group (the other two infantry battalions, two German machine-gun companies and a mountain gun battery) under Major Meyer would remain in reserve.

This plan was exactly what the British were anticipating, but it came at the earliest possible date they were expecting. By now, the two brigades of ANZAC mounted troops had been working on a 48-hour schedule for around two weeks. It was an exhausting schedule, and on the piquet line, the troops were spread perilously thin. Two regiments would hold the line with one in reserve. Each forward regiment had two squadrons on the line with one behind, and one in four of those men would be holding the horses in the rear. This left a line of 6.5km (4 miles) being held effectively by 400 men. The piquet line became a series of four- or eight-man posts 100m or so apart, usually on higher points of ground for better visibility.

When the 2nd Light Horse Brigade (under Colonel John Royston) began to return after dusk on 3 August, it took some hours to filter through the piquet line in small units. The 1st Light Horse Brigade (under Lieutenant-Colonel John Meredith) became aware close to midnight that some of the troops, which they could see in the moonlight and assumed were the other brigade's rearguards, were in fact Ottomans, and sporadic firing began to break out. The firing gradually spread along the whole line as the Ottoman advance guards came into contact and began to attempt to feel their way past the piquets. At around 0100hrs there was a lull, presumably as the commanders in the 2nd and 3rd Ottoman Groups assessed the situation. By now, the 2nd Light Horse Regiment, on the southern end of the line, had called for reinforcements from the 1st Light Horse Regiment in reserve, although it would take considerable time for those reinforcements to arrive. At 0200hrs, the Ottomans renewed their attacks in greater force, and at 0300hrs, they took

Light Horsemen stop for a 'brew' on patrol.

Mount Meredith, a prominence at the junction between the 2nd and 3rd Light Horse Regiments.

With their flanks turned, both regiments began a steady withdrawal to their next positions. It would be an incredible feat of soldering; managing a staged, fighting withdrawal over a broad front at night while in close contact with a vastly superior enemy. Lieutenant Colonel G. Bourne, commanding the 2nd Light Horse Regiment, records in the regimental history:

'The post I occupied during the battle of Romani 8am 4.8.16 to 4am 5.8.16.; Left to right: Cpl Nurse D.W. Williams, E.G.W., Cpl. Ellesdon, Maj. Spragge, Donnelly, Quartley, Sgt. Robertson's boots.' Collection of Edward Williams, Wellington Mounted Rifles. (Auckland War Memorial Museum Tāmaki Paenga Hira, PH-ALB-211-p3-2)

> Which of us will forget the scamper away? How so many did get away is a marvel. The bullets were making little spurts of flame all round and among us, on striking the sand. Here we experienced for the first time, the moral effect of turning our backs on the enemy, and the question arose in our minds as we rode, 'Can we reform?' The order 'Sections about – Action front' was given as we reached the position, and was splendidly carried out.

By 0400hrs or shortly after, the new line was established on the east–west positions as planned, along the front (southern) slope of Wellington Ridge and then west to Mount Royston. It had not been without losses, with some piquets overwhelmed as they retreated, but the sun would rise shortly before 0430hrs on a largely intact 1st Brigade. However, the new position was far from secure. At 0400hrs, an artillery bombardment had opened up on the ridge held by the 52nd Division, and the Ottoman 1st Group, which had already moved close to the line, began to move forward and exploit the gaps and terrain between the redoubts. German aircraft appeared soon after dawn, attacking the camps and troop concentrations behind the ridge, and from around 0700hrs, the artillery began to concentrate on the southern redoubts, on the eastern side of Katib Gannit. Particularly at the southern end of the line, the broken ground allowed small groups of Ottoman troops to begin infiltrating deep into the Scottish lines.

The pressure continued to mount on the ANZACs, and Ottoman artillery that had been moved to Mount Meredith opened fire on their eastern positions soon after dawn. Shortly after 0600hrs, Chauvel ordered his men back over the crest of Wellington Ridge, to dig in on the northern slopes out of direct sight and artillery fire. By now, the 2nd Light Horse Brigade had also entered the fight, after being allowed a few hours rest after its exertions of the previous day. The 6th and 7th Light Horse Regiments had joined the 1st and parts of the 3rd Regiments in the Wellington Ridge area, while the Wellington Mounted Rifles were held as the divisional reserve. The Ottomans also began to push around the open flank west of Mount Royston and at 0530hrs, Lawrence ordered the 5th Mounted Brigade to move across and block the

Bodies and debris left behind after the Battle of Romani.

NIGHT RETREAT, ROMANI, 0200HRS, 4 AUGUST 1916 (PP. 56–57)

In the early hours of 4 August 1916, the 1st Australian Light Horse Brigade conducted perhaps the most difficult military manoeuvre possible: a fighting retreat in the dark while closely engaged with an enemy that greatly outnumbered it. The brigade was widely dispersed over a broad front in small piquets of four to eight men, **(1)** like this one from the 3rd Regiment. No defensive arrangements such as trenches or even scrapes were allowed, in case they betrayed their location to enemy reconnaissance.

Although the piquets were dismounted, their horses were kept close behind and held by one man in four. When hard pressed, most were able to use their superior manoeuvrability to keep ahead of the enemy **(2)**. On foot, the heavily laden Australians **(3)** found themselves at a disadvantage to the Ottomans, who frequently went barefoot in the soft sand, but by using their horses **(4)** to move quickly out of contact the Light Horsemen were able to remain (sometimes literally) one step ahead. Despite the use of the horses, the sheer weight of numbers or occasionally misjudgement led to some piquets being overwhelmed. This was the mounted arms being used to their best effect: remaining mobile to compensate for their relative lack of strength and firepower.

Each man carried basic kit including 90 rounds of ammunition in a bandolier and sometimes a further 50 in a belt pouch **(5)**. Another bandolier of ammunition was carried around his horse's neck, while a greatcoat and ground sheet was rolled up in front of the saddle **(6)**. These men wear the 'flashes' of the 3rd Regiment on their upper arm, and one wears the coveted Light Horse emu feather plume in his slouch hat **(7)**. The Ottoman troops also only carried their basic web equipment for the attack, and over the next day and a half would struggle to replenish their ammunition, water and food.

move, followed two hours later by the New Zealand Mounted Rifles Brigade. After riding into contact with the enemy, the British and New Zealand horsemen would hold them at bay until nearly midday, when they would slowly start to push them back. Finally, at around 1700hrs, a counter-attack led by a mounted charge of Gloucestershire and Worcestershire Yeomen pushed the Ottomans back off the hill and secured the flank. Lieutenant E. T. Cripps of D Squadron RGH described his day in a letter home:

> I and three other troops were told to hold a line of sand, which we did from 9 till 3 [sic] in the blazing sun – fired at the whole time and no target to shoot at within range. We lay in the boiling hot sand and every now and then fired volleys at a stump where there was a sniper… I hated it – nothing to do and being shot at the whole time. But after that we had the show of the war! We were called in, allowed a suck at our bottles, and then off to a flank, to a high sky line. Got shrapnelled on the way… We got on the ridge, which was like a razor back and which the Turks evacuated as we advanced. And down below us in the plain such a scene!… We gave them hell! About 500 surrendered and four guns to us. It was brilliant.

For most of the day, the Wellington Ridge and Katib Gannit areas were the primary cause of concern for both Chauvel and Smith. As the onsite commanders, they were far more in touch with the situation than the distant Lawrence, whose communications were being slowed and interrupted by Ottoman artillery cutting cables and the sheer weight of signals traffic, although they each had their own priorities and perhaps would have benefited from clearer instructions from above. Ottoman infantry and machine gunners lined the crest of Wellington Ridge and could fire down onto the ANZACs and their camp below. Although some well-aimed fire from an Ayrshire Battery in 260th Brigade Royal Artillery would deal with the machine guns, the weight of fire was still considerable, and in the mid-morning, Chauvel appealed to Smith for support. However, Smith had his own concerns. His Nos 3, 4 and 5 Redoubts, east of Katib Gannit, were under heavy attack, as were Nos 1 and 2 to the south of the high ground. These two redoubts, and Nos 21 and 21A to their north-west, were to the south-east of Wellington Ridge, and thus effectively behind Ottoman lines, open to attack from both sides, while Nos 22 and 22A were on or behind the level of Wellington Ridge. These redoubts were all held by the 155th Brigade. The Ottomans were already attempting to infiltrate between the redoubts, and success would enable them to outflank the ANZACs on Wellington Ridge and pierce the British rear.

Smith was already committing parts of his reserve to hold this section, with the 156th Brigade being committed to support Nos 22 and 23 Redoubts, and further troops to support the redoubts to the east. Nos 22, 22A and 23

Members of one of the German machine-gun companies, which were captured almost intact.

Australian Light Horsemen search Ottoman prisoners after the battle.

Redoubts were already providing fire support to the ANZACs, as were his understrength artillery batteries. Smith was forced to refuse the request at that time, and fortuitously the Ottoman assaults on Wellington Ridge began to tail off in the late morning. However, heavy attacks continued on the Scottish redoubts, particularly Nos 4 and 5, which came under heavy bombardment and sustained infantry attack, and of course the fighting at Mount Royston continued.

Colonel John 'Galloping Jack' Royston proved to be an inspiration to his 2nd Light Horse Brigade. The heavy-set, 56-year-old South African veteran of the Zulu and Boer Wars was constantly on the move, apparently running 14 horses into exhaustion during the day. According to the Australian Official History, he constantly exhorted his men to '"Keep your heads down, lads! Stick to it! Stick to it! You are making history today." To one troop he cried: "We are winning now. They are retreating in their hundreds." "And" said one of the light horsemen afterwards, "I poked my head over the top, and there were the blighters coming on in thousands."' Even when wounded he would not slow down, and at 1500hrs, Chauvel had to chase Royston personally so that he could order him to have his wound dressed. Even after that, he would be seen riding along the front line with blood-stained bandages flapping out behind him.

However, the pressure did ease, and the ANZACs were given most of the afternoon to rest after their long, hard fight against superior numbers. Being pushed back to the edges of their own camp had meant that the camp and their horse lines had come under direct fire, but it also meant that hot food

British infantry guarding Ottoman prisoners.

and tea could be brought forward relatively easily. Water was in short supply, so issued in rationed amounts. For the Ottomans, the situation was more difficult. Supplies were limited, and just as the British had been falling back onto their own lines of logistics, so the Ottomans had been moving farther from theirs. It was difficult to bring up sufficient food, water or ammunition to the front lines. Kressenstein also experienced numerous communications issues as he attempted to control a broad battlefield and forces that had run into unexpected resistance. Kressenstein committed at least part of his 4th Group to the fighting, and it may have been this that led to a renewed Ottoman attack on Wellington Ridge at 1730hrs. This was broken up by Scottish artillery and rifle fire from the ANZACs and the redoubts, and at 1845hrs the 1/7th and 1/8th Scottish Rifles advanced from the area of Nos 22A and 23 Redoubts and, supported by the Light Horse on their right, pushed the Ottomans back to the crest of Wellington Ridge before dusk fell at around 2000hrs.

Sporadic firing continued on Wellington Ridge during the night and Ottoman parties maintained their efforts to infiltrate the gap between No. 5 Redoubt and No. 2 to its south, but for the most part both sides were content to break contact. On the British side, the wounded were evacuated to the railhead, troops repaired or improved their positions, and ammunition, water and rations were issued. At Pelusium Station, the first two brigades of the 42nd Division had begun to arrive, they were short of both water and logistical support, and the 3rd Australian Light Horse Brigade also arrived to rejoin its division. Lawrence now ordered preparations for the planned counter-attack to start. At dawn on 5 August, the 156th Brigade and the ANZACs would storm and secure Wellington Ridge, followed by a general advance towards the east by the 52nd Division, an advance by the A&NZ Mounted Division back out to their initial positions, while the 42nd Division, 3rd Light Horse Brigade, 5th Mounted Brigade and NZMR Brigade would all begin to advance into the open Ottoman flank, moving through the other two Light Horse brigades and continuing east. All of the mounted troops would come under Chauvel's command.

Among the Ottoman forces captured after Romani were a complete field ambulance, one of two in the Ottoman 1st Expeditionary Force.

Pursuit from Romani, 7–12 August 1916

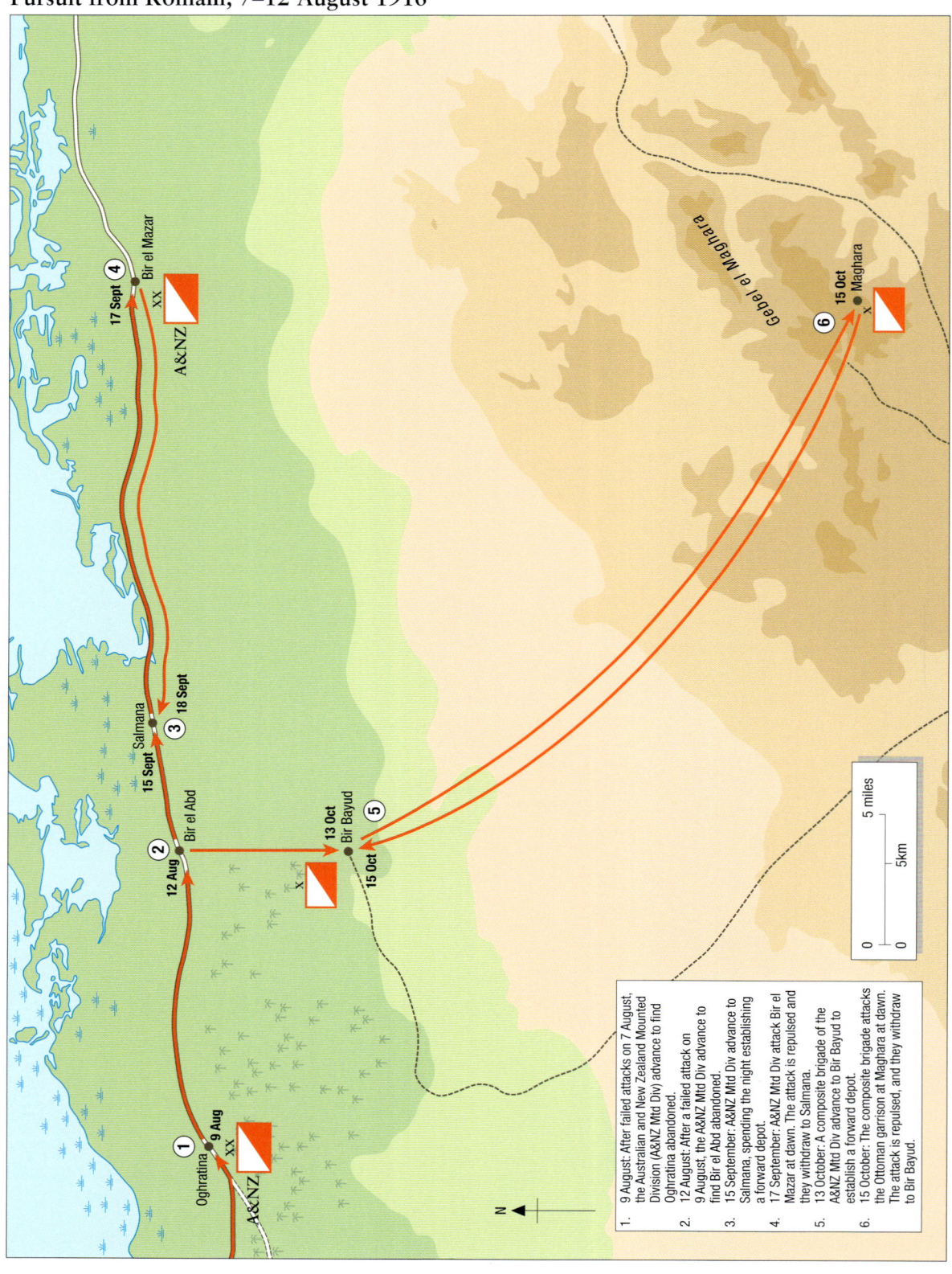

1. 9 August: After failed attacks on 7 August, the Australian and New Zealand Mounted Division (A&NZ Mtd Div) advance to find Oghratina abandoned.
2. 12 August: After a failed attack on 9 August, the A&NZ Mtd Div advance to find Bir el Abd abandoned.
3. 15 September: A&NZ Mtd Div advance to Salmana, spending the night establishing a forward depot.
4. 17 September: A&NZ Mtd Div attack Bir el Mazar at dawn. The attack is repulsed and they withdraw to Salmana.
5. 13 October: A composite brigade of the A&NZ Mtd Div advance to Bir Bayud to establish a forward depot.
6. 15 October: The composite brigade attacks the Ottoman garrison at Maghara at dawn. The attack is repulsed, and they withdraw to Bir Bayud.

PURSUIT FROM ROMANI

In the event, the British plan unravelled almost immediately. Most of the troops were not ready to move at dawn, although the Scots attacked Wellington Ridge as planned. This attack met with an almost instant collapse of the Ottoman forces on the ridge. Overnight, the Ottomans had not been able to resupply their men, and communications remained poor. While the Ottoman soldiery were famous for their stamina and doggedness in battle, they had reached their limit, and nearly 900 surrendered to the advancing Scottish Rifles. Australian horsemen swept forward on their right, and captured 600 more. What was left of the 2nd and 3rd Groups had melted away by 0500hrs, but the British pursuit ran into problems straight away. The 127th Brigade of the 42nd Division began its march, but the soft sand and lack of acclimatization led to it halting after several hours at Hafr Enna before even making contact with the enemy. The 125th Brigade followed several hours later and also made poor progress. Both had lost hundreds of men fallen out from the heat. The Lowlanders suffered a similarly limited advance, slowed by the soft sand, and from around 0630hrs, the bulk of the pursuit fell to the mounted arms.

As the mounted brigades moved forward, they overran numerous small bodies of Ottoman troops. However, in the mid-afternoon, they encountered a formed Ottoman rearguard at Qatia. The three Australian Light Horse brigades and the 5th Mounted Brigade moved in to attack, but were forced to go to ground under heavy fire. Eventually, Chauvel ordered his brigades to break contact and withdraw for the night. The pursuit would recommence the next day, again with a slow infantry advance while the 3rd Light Horse and 5th Mounted Brigades harassed and attacked the retreating

The mounted troops spent the months after Romani at the leading edges of the army, living a rough and ready life. Sores and stomach problems were prevalent. (Trustees of the Queen's Own Worcestershire Hussars Museum)

A patrol from the Wellington Mounted Rifles, looking rough and ready after months in the field. (Auckland War Memorial Museum Tāmaki Paenga Hira, PH-ALB-213-p77-5)

enemy; the 1st and 2nd Light Horse Brigades spent the day resting both horses and men.

The Ottomans had suffered a serious defeat. Kressenstein soundly blamed his Ottoman troops, but managed to hold his remaining forces together admirably. He was now intent on a steady, controlled fighting retreat with the ultimate goal of establishing a defensive line along the Egypt–Palestine border. In the short term, he put up a highly effective rearguard, and while he withdrew from Qatia on the night of 5 August, on the following day he was similarly able to stymie a mounted attack on Oghratina before again withdrawing, this time to Bir el Abd. Here, a large-scale attack by mounted troops was not only stopped on 9 August, but a limited Ottoman counter-attack mounted. Bir el Abd was then abandoned as the Ottomans continued to fall back, and was occupied by the EEF without opposition on 12 August. At this point, Murray called a halt to the pursuit as his advanced troops moved further from their logistics and support. Kressenstein had managed to keep control of his troops and make a successful withdrawal, breaking contact with pursuing forces and without the retreat ever turning into a rout.

The successful withdrawal of the Ottomans after Romani tarnished the overall accomplishment of the EEF, and is a credit to Kressenstein despite a generally poor performance during the battle itself. Kressenstein had fallen into the British trap, largely lost control of his troops, done little to affect events after the battle had opened and would afterwards blame his subordinate officers and men for the outcome. Equally, mistakes had clearly been made on the British side, particularly in their intelligence assessments of the Ottoman strength and timelines (even if their predictions of Kressenstein's plan had been correct) and in the lack of proper preparations for the counter-attack, and some communications issues. However, it remained a resounding victory for the British, and especially the Australian and New Zealand contingents. The EEF suffered approximately 300 officers and men killed (nearly 200 from the A&NZ Mounted Division) and another 900 wounded (650 from the A&NZ Mounted Division). On the other hand, approximately 1,250 Ottoman dead were recovered from the battlefield, another 4,000 taken prisoner, and it is estimated that as many as 4,000 more were wounded or their bodies recovered and buried by the Ottomans – a casualty rate of nearly two-thirds of Kressenstein's force. More indicative, the Ottomans would then stage a steady withdrawal back to Palestine, ceding control of the Sinai Desert to the British, and with it ensuring the security of the Suez Canal. Few other British battles during World War I would be so decisive and clear cut.

Having broken contact with their pursuers, the Ottomans fell steadily back while leaving several small garrisons at key points to delay the EEF. Kressenstein was now intent on establishing a defensive line along the Egypt–Palestine border, anchored at either end by the defences and railheads at Gaza and Beersheba, and Tel el Sharia in the centre. There was some discussion of pulling back further, to a line running from Jaffa

A basic infantry bivouac using blanket shelters. Deep trenches dug under the cover allowed the troops to stay warm in the intense cold of the night and cooler during the heat of the day.

to Jerusalem. Some defensive works were started in the Judean Mountains around the latter city, although these also related to the long-running Ottoman fear that the British and French would use their complete mastery of the Mediterranean to launch amphibious landings against the coasts of Palestine or Syria. Meanwhile, acrimonious arguments among the senior staff of the 1st Expeditionary Force over the causes of the recent defeat led to several senior officers being reassigned. Djemal Pasha broadly sided with Kressenstein in these arguments, undermining his own credibility with his Ottoman officers. Meanwhile, Djemal assigned 4,000 recruits from depots in Jerusalem and Antab to replace losses in the 3rd Infantry Division, and also secured the transfer of the 3rd Cavalry Division (two regiments strong) to the Sinai front.

Murray and Lawrence were largely content to let the Ottomans go. They continued to focus the EEF's efforts on building up the logistical support needed to operate large bodies of troops in the desert effectively. In July, the Imperial War Committee had decided that the best place to establish a forward defensive line was at El Arish, some 153km (95 miles) from the EEF's base depot at Kantara. Maintaining a large enough force at such an extreme distance from their main supply base over desert terrain would be a difficult matter, and while Murray has often been criticized for the slowness of his advance from Romani, the need to keep his troops supplied was an obvious one. The desert would be utterly unforgiving to troops and animals who did not have adequate logistical

A common way to make camps more comfortable was to dig long parallel trenches, allowing the area in between to serve as a table.

support. The railway continued to make progress, but water remained a more serious problem.

By the end of June, some 136,000 litres (30,000 gallons) of water were being delivered to Romani every day. However, much of it was needed by the railway engines that drew it, and each man required at least 4.5 litres (1 gallon) and each horse 23 litres (5 gallons) per day to survive. The one mounted and two infantry divisions in the desert, plus the logistics troops who maintained the railway and lines of supply, would require over one million litres (225,000 gallons) per day at full strength, although admittedly most were not.

In the Qatia basin, additional water was relatively easy to find, if not always in sufficient quantities or speeds. To draw enough water from a well for a regiment of horsemen took time, and considerable effort was put into developing the wells and cisterns already behind British lines. For troops on patrol, the introduction of the Spearpoint Pump did a great deal to alleviate the problem. Modified versions of the British Army pumps, more commonly known as Abyssinia Wells or Norton Tubes, were first introduced by Lieutenant Colonel Lachlan Wilson, commanding officer of the 5th Light Horse Regiment, in the Sinai. Essentially a 3m (10ft) long perforated tube, it could tap into underground water without the need to dig a hole. Two men could hammer a tube deep enough to strike water in 30 minutes, which would otherwise take several hours to reach by digging. A 'lift and force' pump would then draw the water up and into canvas troughs, or cisterns at more permanent sites, created by building sandbag walls and lining the inside with canvas sheets. However, the further east the EEF advanced, the harder it was to find water, and what was found was more saline and poorer in quality. Murray and his senior officers had to be careful not to overreach, and lose troops and animals through lack of proper water supply.

The bulk of EEF logistics still relied on the animals and men of the Egyptian Labour Corps and the Camel Transport Corps.

The eastern Sinai Desert, late 1916

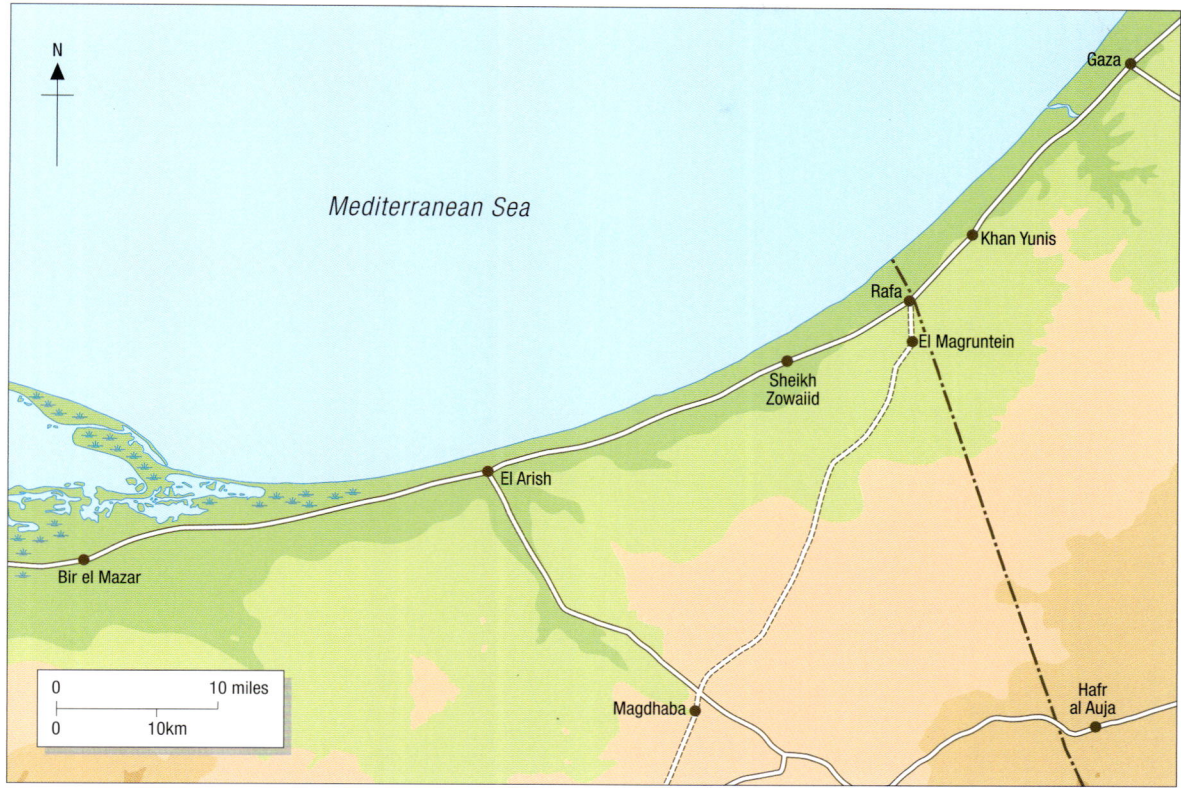

BIR EL MAZAR

In early September, the EEF's patrols were reaching Bir el Mazar, located on the coast about halfway between Bir el Abd and El Arish. The Ottomans had left a garrison here, variously estimated at between 500 and 2,400 strong. Chauvel was ordered to advance on and attack the enemy post. Intelligence was minimal, with few firm details on the strength of the enemy (although Chauvel's most recent information was to expect 2,200–2,300 infantry from the 31st and 39th Regiments, 10 machine guns and four mountain guns, which was broadly correct) or their exact locations. A local guide was provided but proved of little use. Chauvel's orders were also vague; he was to attack and capture Bir el Mazar if possible, but if the enemy was found to be stronger than anticipated or little progress had been made by 0600hrs (an hour or so after the intended starting time), he was to withdraw. Much longer and the health of his horses would begin to suffer adversely, leaving his troops immobile and vulnerable.

A force consisting of the three brigades of the A&NZ Mounted Division advanced to Salmana, 32km (20 miles) west of Bir el Mazar, on the night of 15/16 September, where a convoy of 700 camels deposited 64,000 litres (14,000 gallons) of water to augment the local wells. On the same night, two British aircraft bombed the German aerodrome at El Arish with the intention

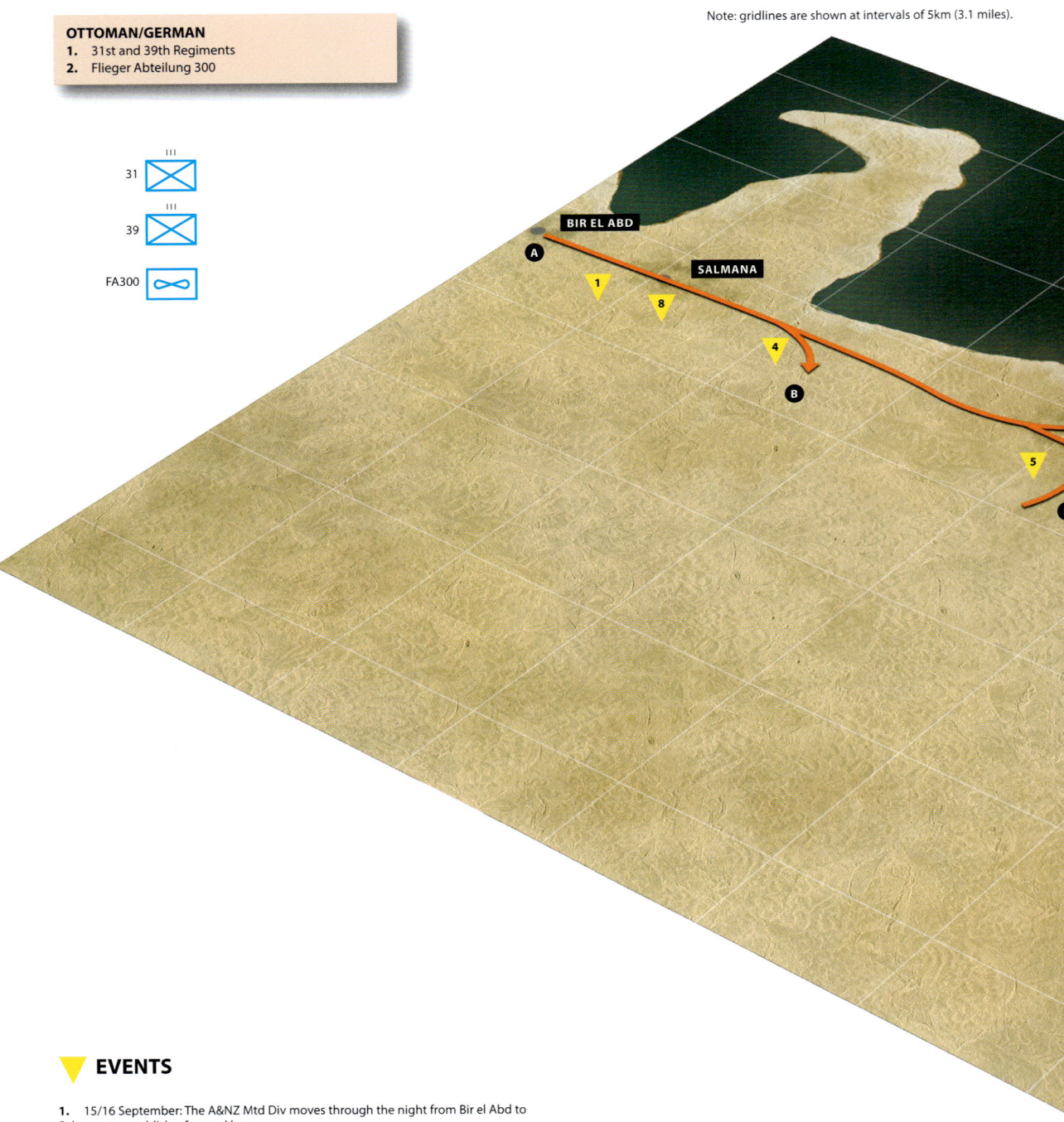

OTTOMAN/GERMAN
1. 31st and 39th Regiments
2. Flieger Abteilung 300

EVENTS

1. 15/16 September: The A&NZ Mtd Div moves through the night from Bir el Abd to Salmana to establish a forward base.

2. 15/16 September: The Royal Flying Corps attack the German air base at El Arish to disrupt the German ability to conduct reconnaissance patrols.

3. 0530hrs onwards, 16 September: The Royal Flying Corps mounts patrols between Bir el Mazar and El Arish to keep German aircraft away. The plan has mixed success.

4. 2030hrs: The A&NZ Mtd Div leaves Salmana after dusk to march to Bir el Mazar. The 1st Light Horse Brigade moves out last and sets up in supporting positions between the two towns.

5. 0500hrs, 17 September: The British attack Bir el Mazar at dawn. The 3rd Light Horse Brigade swings around to attack from the south-east, and the 2nd Light Horse Brigade attacks from the west. A battalion of the Imperial Camel Corps advances from the south but does not make contact.

6. 0530hrs: Two formations of East Indies and Egypt Seaplane Squadron aircraft approach El Arish to direct the guns of warships offshore. One fails to find the target, the other is intercepted by German aircraft.

7. 0630hrs: German aircraft, having chased off the floatplanes, attack the British flotilla.

8. 0945hrs: The attacking brigades begin to break off contact, and withdraw through the day back to Salmana.

ATTACK ON BIR EL MAZAR, 15–17 SEPTEMBER 1916

The EEF attempted to coordinate a three-dimensional attack – staged with air, land and sea forces across large areas and over several days – with limited success. Ultimately, the technology and communications were lacking, but most importantly the Ottoman and German defenders were too strong.

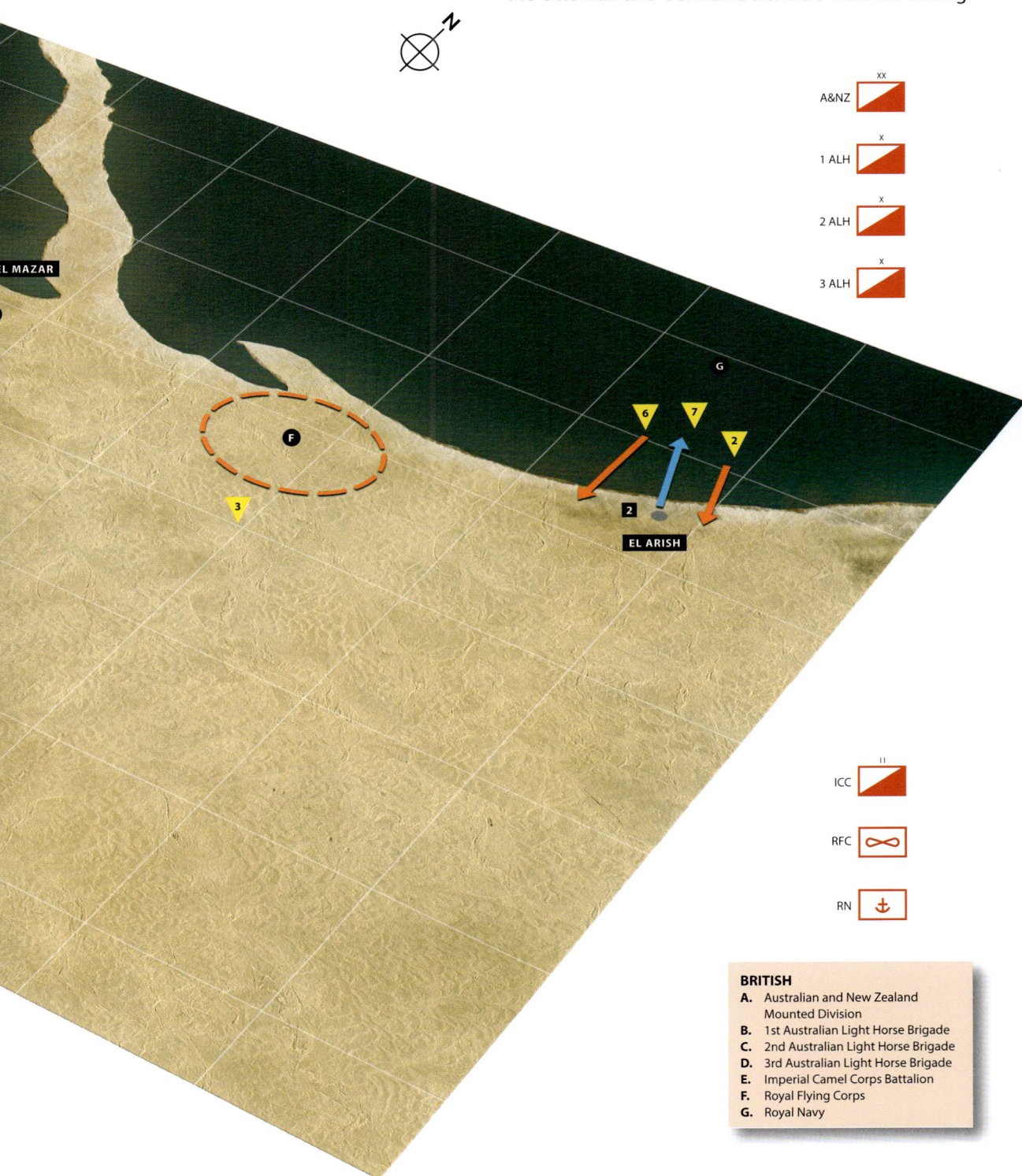

BRITISH
A. Australian and New Zealand Mounted Division
B. 1st Australian Light Horse Brigade
C. 2nd Australian Light Horse Brigade
D. 3rd Australian Light Horse Brigade
E. Imperial Camel Corps Battalion
F. Royal Flying Corps
G. Royal Navy

The water supply was still largely based on camels carrying tin 'fanatis', containing 45–55 litres (10–12 gallons) each, from the railhead to the advanced units.

of keeping the Germans grounded and preventing them from spotting the gathered troops. Throughout the following day, the troops remained hidden as much as possible under cover, and the RFC put up constant patrols of two aircraft at a time over the area to again try to keep FA300 away. This plan failed quite early in the day, soon after the second patrol took over at around 0730hrs. One of the two aircraft, a DH1a, was forced to land with engine trouble. Two German aircraft then attacked and forced down the second machine, a Martinsyde Elephant flown by No. 14 Squadron's commanding officer, Major Ballantyne. The German aircraft were able to locate, and strafe, the partially hidden Australian troops.

Regardless of being discovered, the 2nd and 3rd Light Horse Brigades left Salmana overnight, leaving the 1st Brigade to provide guards for the water stores and then move up in support, forming a screen to cover their rear and their retreat. The 2nd Brigade was to advance on Bir el Mazar from the west and the 3rd Brigade was to circle around to attack from the south-east, while also being prepared to round up the garrison if it tried to escape. Two troops of RHA were to support the attack, while three Australian companies of the ICC supported by two guns of the Hong Kong and Singapore (HK&S) Mountain Battery, were supposed to sweep out of the desert to the south. In the event, communications broke down, the cameliers never made contact and the artillery became lost. As dawn on 17 September broke in thick fog, several Australian units stumbled into contact with Ottoman outposts, which were well dug in on high ground.

After a short period of sporadic fighting, in which some small gains were made, Chauvel ordered a retreat, to the bitterness of some of his subordinates. With a scattered and incomplete force at his disposal and an enemy force not much smaller than his own, well dug in and on full alert, an easy victory was unlikely. The taking of Bir el Mazar would not be worth the casualties it could cost. Chauvel pulled his force back to Salmana, where the watering of the horses rapidly dissolved into chaos. There was already too little water to give each man and horse a full ration anyway, but the system broke down and some units had to go completely

Comforts and entertainment were sparse in the desert. Some canteens and occasional concert parties were available nearer the railhead.

unwatered. Chauvel then withdrew his whole force back to the main EEF lines at Bir el Abd.

During the day of the attack, the Royal Navy had launched its own attack on El Arish in an attempt to divert Ottoman forces and keep FA300 away from Bir el Mazar. Two formations of floatplanes, each consisting of a Short 184 escorted by two single seaters, operating from HMS *Ben-My-Chree*, were to direct the fire of HMS *Espiegle* and the monitors *M15* and *M31* against targets at El Arish. One formation encountered light ground fire, but could not find any targets and returned to their ship, where one aircraft was lost on landing. The other formation was attacked by Rumplers from FA300. The two escorting aircraft (one Sopwith Schneider and one Sopwith Baby) both turned to protect the Short 184 despite being clearly outclassed. The Short 184 managed to escape, but both of the escorts were lost, with one of the pilots killed. The Germans then proceeded to attack the naval flotilla in what they would call the 'Sea Battle of El Arish'. The action proved that the already outdated seaplanes, further hampered by their large and ungainly floats, were no match for the German aircraft, and the RNAS would increasingly begin to move their operations further north to less well-defended coasts, well away from the Sinai.

The A&NZ Mounted Division returned to camp to recover from the strains of operating for an extended period in the desert in summer temperatures with inadequate water. A few days later, the Ottomans withdrew their garrison from Bir el Mazar. A month later, another, albeit smaller scale, raid was mounted against a second Ottoman garrison at Maghara. Located about 80km (50 miles) south-east of Romani, this garrison sat in the foothills of the Gebel el Maghara mountains that dominated the central route across the Sinai. This time, better preparations were made. The RFC photographed the Ottoman positions, and these were used to produce maps. An advanced landing ground

A bivouac camp of the 231st Field Ambulance uses the available cover, nestling under scrub.

was established at Salmana, from where aircraft made regular patrols during the course of the attack, dropping messages to the attacking troops.

A smaller, and thus more easily supplied, strike force was assembled. The column consisted of the 11th and 12th Light Horse Regiments and the 1st City of London Yeomanry, supported by 300 cameliers and two guns from the HK&S Mountain Battery, all under the command of Major-General Alister Dallas. It totalled approximately 1,400 troops, which after the removal of horse-holders left around 1,100 for the actual attack. To support them, nearly 3,000 logistical personnel and 7,000 camels were needed, carrying water and rations for 4–5 days. They deployed forward on the night of 13/14 October to Bir Bayud, where wells had previously been developed. Although this was roughly halfway to Maghara in a direct line, the route of march from Bir Bayud to the objective was closer to 56km (35 miles). This longer march was made on the night of 14/15 October, with the force arriving at Maghara at dawn.

Dallas was operating under the same orders as Chauvel had been, to withdraw if serious opposition was met. Again, heavy fog was encountered, and the 11th Light Horse Regiment opened the attack by stumbling into Ottoman piquets on the high ground above them, which the Light Horsemen immediately charged. The Ottomans were pushed from their position, and the 11th continued to push directly ahead while the 12th Regiment and Yeomen worked around to the flank. After two hours, the main Ottoman position was in sight and the junior commanders in the units were confident that it could be captured without heavy loss. However, Dallas was conscious of his orders and that a combination of the highly broken ground and lingering fog meant that parts of the battlefield were still obscured and communications

A DH1a from No. 14 Squadron. Although the RFC received more modern aircraft through the summer of 1916, these still struggled against their Germans opponents.

A patrol from No. 6 Company, 2nd Battalion, Imperial Camel Corps.

were difficult. It would be too easy for Ottoman forces to approach unseen and infiltrate between his units. At 1000hrs, he called off the attack, and the force fell back to Bir Bayud. This time the logistical arrangements were much better, and the whole force was successfully watered.

As at Bir el Mazar, after the action at Maghara some officers and men expressed frustration at being recalled when progress appeared to be being made. However, Murray's orders were clear, and both Chauvel and Dallas were correct to follow them. Horses and men were already suffering from extended periods on limited water in the heat and sand of the Sinai, and getting embroiled in a lengthy fight during the heat of the day could have a serious effect on their health. Victories over small Ottoman garrisons, which were likely to withdraw anyway, were not worth the risk of losing, even if for a short period, a major part of the EEF's main striking forces. Chauvel would face the same dilemma again before the end of the campaign.

On 23 October 1916, the EEF underwent a reorganization. Murray moved his headquarters from Ismailia to Cairo, to be in better touch with the civil government in Egypt and the other areas for which he was responsible. At Ismailia, the headquarters of the Eastern Force stood up under Lieutenant-General Sir Charles Dobell, with responsibility for the defences of the Canal. The following month more changes came as Nos 1 and 2 Sections of the Canal Defences were merged into the Southern Canal Section, and No. 3 Section became the Northern one. The forces deployed in the Sinai, now some distance away from the rest of their section, were removed to become the independent Desert Column. The Northern Canal Section retained responsibility for the lines of communications and supply for the forces in the Sinai as far as Romani initially, and later El Arish. On 7 December, Lieutenant-General Sir Philip Chetwode arrived from the Western Front to take command of the Desert Column.

A Sopwith Baby being hoisted aboard in the Dardanelles. The pilot, American John Thearsby Bankes-Price, was killed during the 'Sea Battle of El Arish' in September.

While the north-eastern Sinai continued to be the focus of operations, some small-scale raids were also mounted in the south by forces of British Yeomanry and infantry striking at minor Ottoman garrisons at Bir el Tawal, and in December, through the Mitla Pass to Nekhl. Constant ICC patrolling in the mountains and the Sinai Peninsula further south continued to limit Ottoman operations by intercepting their supply columns and cutting their communications, isolating the small Ottoman garrisons and forcing them to withdraw. One of these patrols in early August saw a rare occasion of mounted action for the cameliers. Geoffrey Inchbald would record:

> The Camel Corps scouts suddenly came upon a small enemy ammunition and baggage column consisting of thirty pack mules, a troop of cavalry and about eighty dismounted men, who were crossing an open stretch of ground. The Camel Corps had part of two companies, approximately seventy men in all, a third of whom were ordered to dismount and give covering fire while the remainder, taking advantage of the confusion, charged in extended formation, yelling and firing their rifles from the saddle in the approved Arab style. Needless to say they did not hit anything but, although the Turks put up some slight resistance and managed to get some of their pack animals away, most of them were finally rounded up and surrendered.

Elsewhere in the north, while the mounted troops continued to be highly active, the growing logistics network required guarding against Ottoman or Bedouin raiders who might strike at the railway, pipeline or isolated depots. Guarding these lines and the forward railhead fell to the infantry,

East Indies and Egypt Seaplane Squadron personnel pose with their Short 184 at their Port Said base. While a highly capable aircraft, floatplanes were naturally of lower performance than landplanes.

whose relative lack of mobility made them more suited to static defences. The historian of the 5th Highland Light Infantry would record:

> Bir el Abd was now the most forward infantry post. It was half-way between Kantara and el Arish – so that the 'spear head' of the offensive defensive was making good progress. It was defended by a great ring of outpost positions, each held by a platoon or so, usually with another platoon in support. Night after night we slept in clothes and boots, with our equipment on us, and woke at intervals to peer into the dark for an hour, or see that others peered – then two more hours' sleep and another turn of duty – and so on till we were called for stand-to – variously at three, four, five, or six am, as the season changed. Then we all stood ready, rifles loaded and bayonets fixed, denied cigarettes or conversation, lest our positions be given away to an approaching enemy, who would not naturally be familiar with them as he would in trench warfare, till at last the desolate world revealed itself, empty as ever and, to the jaundiced eye of a fasting man, utterly abominable.

BORDER BATTLES

The Desert Column was now within striking distance of El Arish, and had the necessary logistics to sustain it during the endeavour. The advanced British forces had managed to send small patrols as far as, or even beyond, El Arish. However, the 32–40km (20–25 miles) of desert in between remained almost entirely waterless, while the Ottomans had enveloped all of the sources there with their defences, which were 6.5km (4 miles) deep from the outposts back to their third line. Wells had been dug wherever water could be found within the Desert Column's area of control, but water in large quantities still needed to be hauled 24km (15 miles) from the railhead, while the water pipeline was further back still. Each division of the column by then had some 3,000 camels at its disposal to carry water with it as it advanced – an improvement, but still short of their actual needs. Careful preparations had to be made. As it was, the 42nd Division would have to remain at Bir el Mazar while the A&NZ Mounted Division, 52nd Division and Imperial Camel Corps made the attack.

During the day of 20 December, the RFC began to bring back reports that the Ottoman presence at El Arish was rapidly shrinking, with the tents of the hospital and garrison being pulled down. As preparations were suitably advanced, on the night of 20 December, the mounted troops moved into the desert, followed more slowly by the infantry. At least then, the desert was fading out and the footing becoming more solid, and easier and quicker to march across. By the following day, El Arish had been surrounded, and patrols discovered the Ottoman defences and installations had been abandoned. Not only did the capture of El Arish provide access to considerable water sources, the mouth of the Wadi El Arish provided an area of sheltered water, and within days, supplies were being landed by boat from ships offshore. On 22 December, both General Chetwode and the 52nd Division arrived at El Arish.

In fact, the Ottomans had begun to withdraw their troops and materiel from El Arish on 17 December. After much debate, the Gaza–Beersheba defensive line idea had finally been settled upon. Djemal Pasha had been reluctant to completely abandon the Sinai Desert for political reasons. Equally, neither Djemal nor Kressenstein wanted to abandon entirely the massive investments that had been made in building up the transport network and logistics in the region, while the successful fending off of the attacks on Bir el Mazar and Maghara encouraged the impression that relatively isolated posts could be maintained in the desert. However, the relentless advance of the EEF had eroded this idea, and on 4 December 1916, the decision was made to pull back all of the outposts still left in the desert. The bases at El Arish and Hafr al Auja, at the eastern ends of the northern and central routes across the Sinai respectively, were ordered

The remains of Ottoman trenches at El Arish, sometime after the capture of the town.

Egyptian labourers work on extending the railway to El Arish while others unload supply boats landed from supply ships in the roadstead.

to be withdrawn, leaving only the large (battalion-sized) outposts at Magdhaba and El Magruntein (just south of Rafa, and commonly known in British sources by that name). These too were to be withdrawn, but again the politics of having to pull back the last Ottoman presence in Egypt made Djemal hesitate.

This hesitation would prove disastrous for both garrisons. Acting with perhaps uncharacteristic speed after their long slog from Romani (although the secure logistics base at El Arish may have allowed them greater freedom of movement), Chetwode ordered an immediate pursuit of the withdrawing garrison by the A&NZ Mounted Division, mostly likely to the east towards Rafa. However, within hours reconnaissance reports from the RFC were indicating that the garrison at Magdhaba, 40km (25 miles) south-east of El Arish, was still present in strength, and was possibly being reinforced either by troops from El Arish or from the small posts in the central Sinai that were being dislodged by aggressive patrolling by the Southern Canal Section. General Chauvel was now given a new objective, to capture the garrison at Magdhaba, judged to be around 1,600 Ottoman infantry (their actual strength was nearer 1,400).

There was no time for any special preparations to be made to support the division in this action, which would involve an 80km (50-mile) round march and a day's fighting. Again, water would be the limiting factor. Although the division's camel train could carry a certain amount, the action would need to be decided by the early afternoon or disaster could ensue. Chauvel marched his force – the 1st and 3rd Light Horse Brigades, the NZMR Brigade and the ICC Brigade supported by the Somerset and Inverness Batteries RHA and the HK&S Mountain Battery – through the night in freezing temperatures, halting 6.5km (4 miles) short of his objective at 0500hrs to have breakfast and wait for dawn. A mixture of RFC and AFC aircraft had bombed the garrison on 22 December, and returned at dawn on 23 December to do so again, while also taking closer note of the locations of the Ottoman positions.

OTTOMAN
1–5. One infantry company in each redoubt
6. Battery of mountain artillery

Note: gridlines are shown at intervals of 2km (1.2 miles).

▼ EVENTS

1. 0450hrs: The A&NZ Mtd Div arrives outside Magdhaba, which is garrisoned by five companies of Ottoman infantry and an artillery battery spread across five redoubts and some trench systems.

2. 0800hrs: After air and ground reconnaissance, the A&NZ Mtd Div deploys around the garrison.

3. 0925hrs: General Chaytor, commanding the NZMR and 3rd Light Horse Brigades, deploys his troops. While the NZMR prepare to attack, Chaytor leads the 10th Light Horse Regiment in a wide flanking manoeuvre, while the rest of the brigade is held in reserve. The 10th eventually attacks No. 4 Redoubt.

4. 0955hrs: The New Zealanders begin their advance, and the British artillery opens fire.

5. 1000hrs: The 1st Light Horse Brigade and Imperial Camel Corps Brigade begin to attack along the wadi from the west.

6. 1200hrs: The rest of the 3rd Light Horse Brigade is committed to supporting the New Zealand attack.

7. 1415hrs: The 3rd Light Horse Regiment and elements of the ICC storm and capture No. 1 Redoubt.

8. 1600hrs: No. 2 Redoubt also falls, and the A&NZ Mtd Div pours into the Magdhaba garrison, attacking the other redoubts from the rear.

9. 1630hrs: Colonel Khadir Bey orders the surrender of his remaining troops.

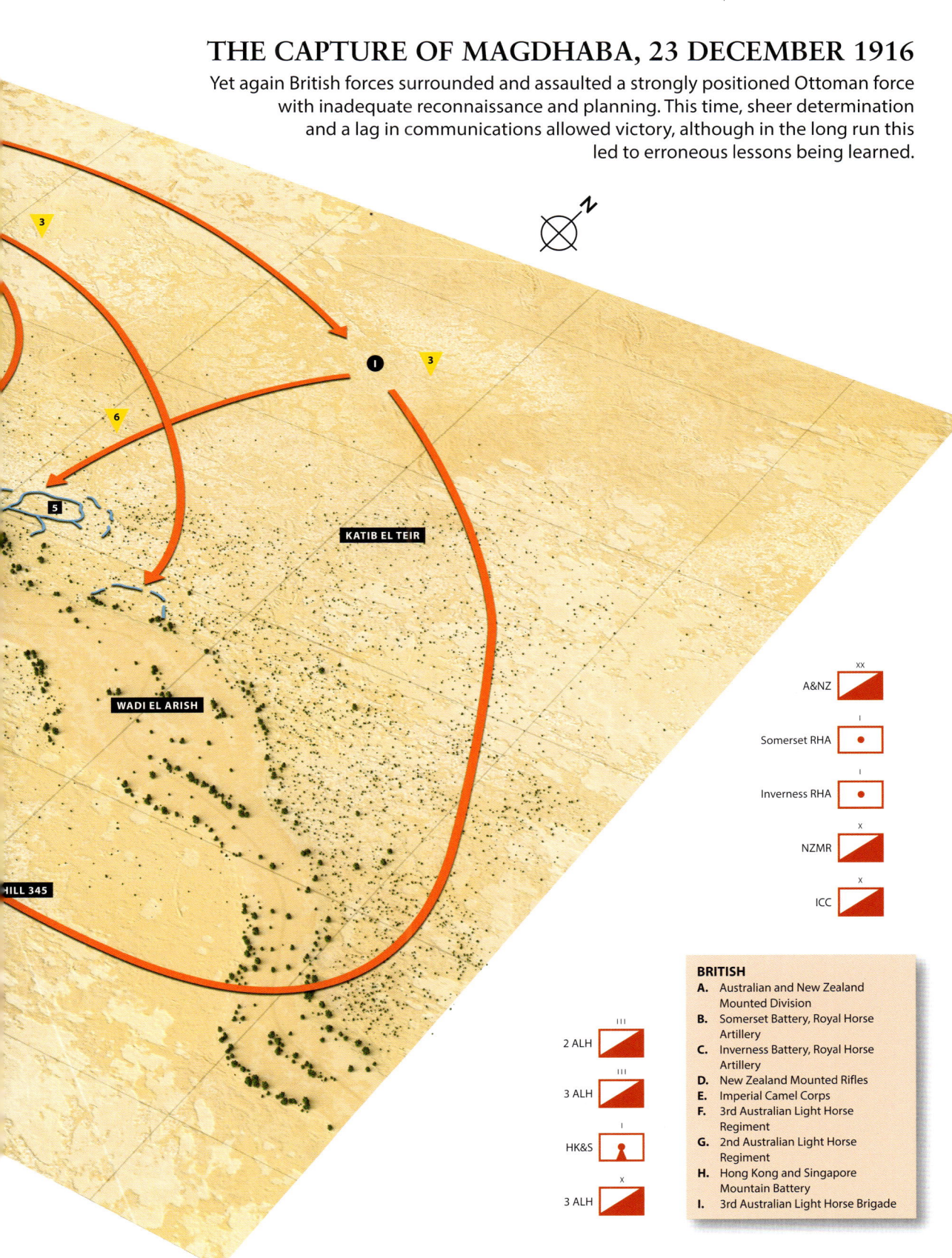

By 0800hrs, air-dropped reports had given Chauvel the information he needed. The Ottoman positions consisted of five main redoubts straddling the roughly east–west running Wadi El Arish. Two redoubts were on the northern bank and three on the south, with smaller trench systems connecting them. The whole position was about 3km (2 miles) long. Unknown to Chauvel, these were held by five companies of the 2nd and 3rd Battalions 80th Regiment under Colonel Khadir Bey, supported by a single mountain battery of four guns, and hampered by a lack of signal wire that made communications across the positions very difficult. However, the redoubts themselves were extremely well sited and built, blending into the terrain and offering excellent fields of fire.

Chauvel ordered his troops to deploy. General Edward Chaytor took his own NZMR Brigade and the 3rd Light Horse Brigade to positions north of Magdhaba. He committed his own brigade to attacking the northern defences, and ordered most of the Light Horse to stay in reserve apart from the 10th Light Horse Regiment, which he led around in a long flanking march, capturing a number of Ottomans as they crossed the Wadi and then attacking the easternmost of the southern redoubts. The ICC Brigade and the 1st Light Horse Brigade were committed to attacking directly from the west, riding to within about 1.5km (1 mile) of No. 1 Redoubt before being forced to dismount and take cover. Spread out and with only limited artillery, at no point did Chauvel's forces have the weight of numbers or firepower to supress the Ottoman defences effectively, and only slow, crawling advances could be made. Lack of precise-enough intelligence and the effects of mirages meant that what artillery the British had deployed could not be used effectively to target Ottoman positions.

Khadir Bey and the staff of the 80th Infantry Regiment at Magdhaba. (Library of Congress Prints and Photographs Division)

At about midday, the rest of the 3rd Light Horse Brigade was committed to attack from the north and north-east, but just over an hour later, Chauvel received word from a party of engineers who had been left about halfway between El Arish and Magdhaba. They had been tasked with digging into the bed of the wadi to prepare a watering station for the force, but reported that no water had been found. Weighing his options, Chauvel was mindful that already the long march home would likely have a detrimental effect on the health of his horses, seriously affecting the strength of his division for days if not weeks to come. He signalled Chetwode shortly before 1400hrs that he intended to withdraw. Orders were sent out to his brigade commanders, but when his messenger arrived at Brigadier-General Charles Cox's position in the Wadi, where his 3rd Light Horse Regiment was now only 90m (100yds) from No. 1 Redoubt and were in close touch with the cameliers on his left, Cox thrust the order back at him declaring 'Take that damned thing away, and let me see it for the first time in half-an-hour.' Within moments, the 3rd Light Horse and Nos 1 and 11 (Australian) Companies of the ICC surged into No. 1 Redoubt, capturing and establishing a foothold inside the Ottoman positions. Chauvel rescinded his orders and renewed his attacks.

Taking advantage of more broken terrain, the 10th Light Horse Regiment was able to close on Nos 3 and 4 Redoubts to the south, and even make a small mounted charge straight through No. 3 and out the far side. Both redoubts fell soon after, and at 1600hrs, No. 2 Redoubt, under the personal command of Khadir Bey, surrendered. By 1630hrs, all resistance had ended, and the Australians and New Zealanders had rounded up nearly 1,300 prisoners, while around 100 Ottoman bodies were recovered and buried. The attackers had lost 22 officers and men killed and 124 wounded. Limited watering of the horses was also able to take place.

Chauvel withdrew his force overnight, albeit leaving medical detachments (guarded by the Auckland Mounted Rifles) to continue to collect and stabilize the wounded. After 30 hours of riding and fighting with limited water, most of the troops were exhausted. Even Chauvel himself fell asleep on the march, dreaming that he was on a foxhunt and waking to find that he had galloped away from the marching column chased by some of his staff officers.

The Desert Column rested at El Arish over Christmas and the New Year. Although it had moved into gentler country, with the soft sands of the Sinai starting to give way to more solid footing and even limited agricultural land, it was still an uncomfortable Christmas. The railway continued to lag behind (it would not reach El Arish until early February 1917) and the edge of the winter rainy season that lashed Palestine led to a cold and wet time for men acclimatized to the baking desert. The winter weather also prevented ships from using the

An Ottoman mountain battery prepares for action.

shallow roadstead offshore, and it took time for the logistics to be built up to support the final step of the campaign.

A single Ottoman garrison remained south of the Gaza–Beersheba line, at El Magruntein. What would effectively be the last action of the 1916 campaign was delayed until an attacking force was despatched on the afternoon of 8 January 1917 to capture it. Under the personal command of General Chetwode, it was a larger force than had been sent against Magdhaba. Chauvel again led a depleted A&NZ Mounted Division with the 1st and 3rd Light Horse Brigades and the NZMR Brigade (supported by the Leicester, Inverness and Somerset Batteries RHA), while Chetwode commanded the ICC Brigade (supported by the HK&S Mountain Battery), the 5th Mounted Brigade (supported by 'B' Battery HAC) and No. 7 Light Car Patrol, consisting of four Model T Ford cars mounted with machine guns, plus support vehicles.

Marching through the night and establishing a supply dump at Sheikh Zowaiid to hold the reserve ammunition and other supplies around 16km (10 miles) from the objective, the force arrived close to the border with Palestine at around 0330hrs on 9 January. While the rest of the force waited for dawn, the NZMR Brigade was sent east to seize the police post at Rafa and occupy several Arab villages between El Magruntein and Gaza. Although this task would not be completed until late morning, in the process, they became the first British troops to enter Palestine, and the subsequent action would be fought straddling two continents, Africa and Asia.

A Light Horseman escorts a local guide at Rafa.

The Ottoman forces at El Magruntein consisted of five companies of the 31st Regiment and a single mountain gun battery, recently reinforced by three machine-gun companies and a dismounted camel company. A central fortified position known as the Reduit stood on conical high ground about 60m (200ft) above the surrounding area with an outlying post, Point 265, to its north, and a semi-circle of three redoubts to the south. Again, they were superbly sited, with low profiles and clear fields of fire for up to 2km (1.2 miles) in all directions, although a complete lack of barbed wire was a definite weakness.

At dawn, and again after reconnaissance reports from the RFC and AFC (this time by wireless to Chetwode's headquarters rather than air-dropped messages), the British forces were deployed, encircling the Ottoman positions. The ICC Brigade, 1st and 3rd Light Horse Brigades were spread out to the south, attacking the three redoubts. The NZMR Brigade was to the north and east, and the 5th Mounted Brigade to the south-west and west, although it took until after midday for these northern and western forces to reach their positions and complete

The action at El Magruntein/Rafa, 9 January 1917

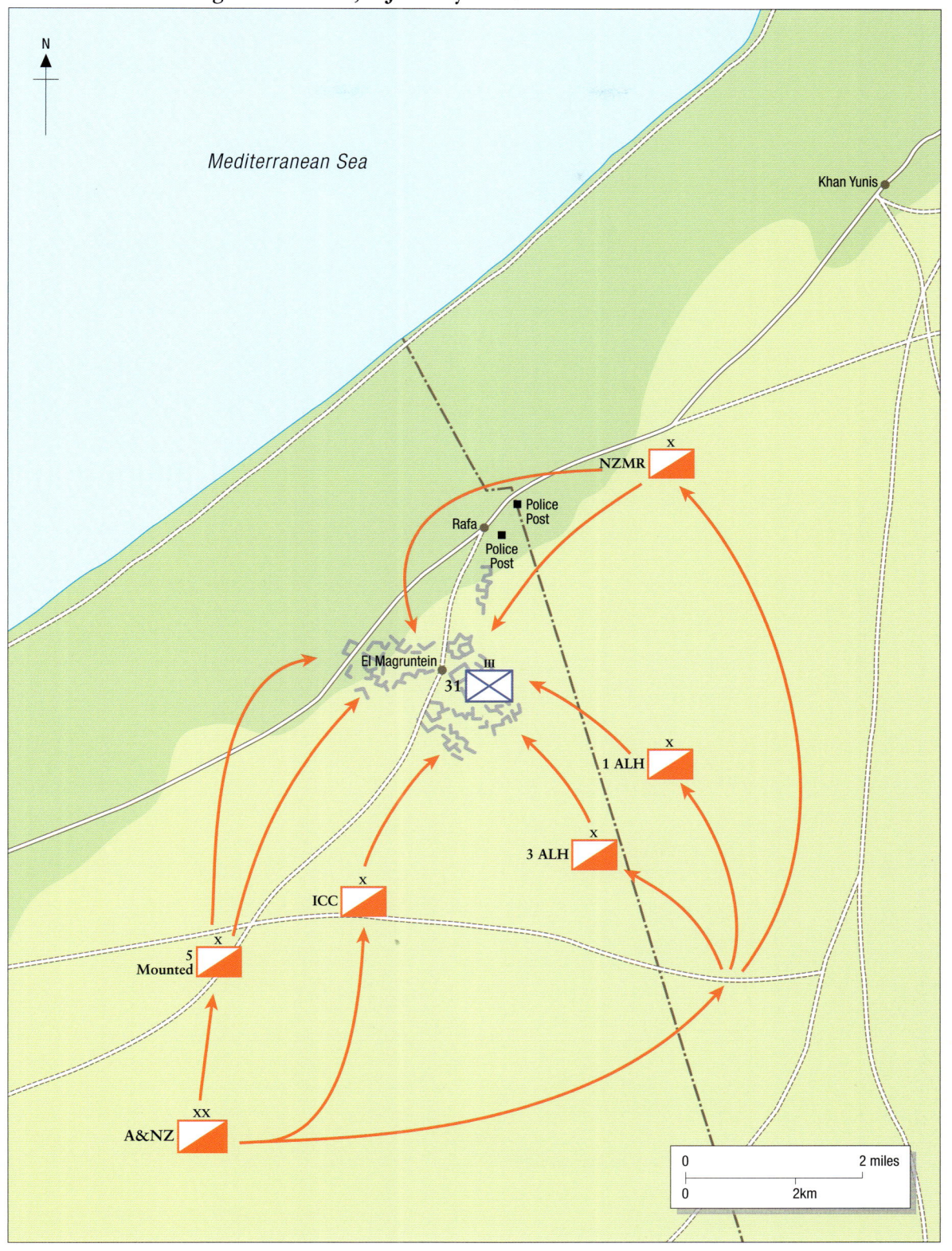

the encirclement. Meanwhile, at 0830hrs, the artillery had opened fire in the south, followed at 0900hrs by an advance by the Australians, who dismounted at 2km (1.2 miles) from their objectives to advance, under heavy fire, on foot. The regimental history of the Canterbury Mounted Rifles records their own similar, slightly later, attack:

> The advance was slow but steady, the men advancing on foot as though they were carrying out manoeuvres. Everything worked like clockwork. A troop would rise from the ground and, covered by the fire of their comrades on either flank, dash forward a few yards, the men throwing themselves down, and bringing fire to bear on the trench in front of them till the remaining troops had come into line.

As at Magdhaba, the attacking forces were spread thinly and lacked the weight of either numbers or firepower to supress or overwhelm the Ottoman defenders effectively at any one point. Although the RFC and AFC were better able to direct the artillery fire through wireless stations attached to the batteries, and the light cars were able to provide localized and limited support by driving in and out of the forward positions to add their machine guns to the covering fire, it was still all too limited, as was the ammunition supply. As early as 1330hrs, the machine guns of the NZMR Brigade were running out of ammunition, and at 1530hrs, the Inverness Battery also had to cease fire. The other batteries and the Light Car Patrol also ran short, and while further stocks were brought up from Sheikh Zowaiid, the 32km (20-mile) round trip took time. Meanwhile, the troops met with limited success, taking a few outer defence works, and in the north managing to get within 550–730m (600–800yds) of the Reduit. However, by 1600hrs, both the aircraft and patrols were reporting Ottoman reinforcements advancing from Khan Yunis in the north and Shellal in the east.

The famous border posts at Rafa, first crossed by the New Zealand Mounted Rifles early on 9 January 1917.

With the troops and horses having been marching and fighting for 24 hours without significant water resupply, limited success, ammunition shortages and enemy reinforcements arriving, Chetwode decided to issue the order the withdraw. The orders reached the 5th Mounted Brigade, the closest unit, quite quickly, but took longer to be passed to the cameliers, New Zealanders and Australians. Again, this delay gave the opportunity for victory to be snatched from defeat and overcome the effects of poor tactics and planning. Before the order could arrive, the NZMR swept over the top of Point 265, and then on into the Reduit itself. From there, they began to assault the eastern-most redoubt from the rear, causing enough of a distraction for the 3rd Light Horse Brigade to storm and capture it from the front. As this redoubt fell, the 5th Mounted and ICC Brigades reversed their withdrawal, charging back into action and capturing the central and western redoubts.

Dusk was approaching, as were further Ottoman troops. Detachments of Australians and New Zealanders were sent to engage and harass the enemy, while the 3rd Light Horse Field Ambulance, guarded by the 8th Light Horse Regiment, remained to gather the wounded. The rest of the force withdrew to Sheikh Zowaiid to resupply and water their horses, taking with them over 1,600 Ottoman prisoners. A further 200 Ottoman dead were recovered, while Chetwode's force had suffered 71 officers and men killed, 415 wounded and one missing. The following morning, the 7th Light Car Patrol and some Australian troops were sent back to El Magruntein to assist in the evacuation of the wounded, and it was found that the Ottoman relief columns had turned back. The last Australians did not leave El Magruntein until midday on 10 January, to make the long march back to El Arish.

Both of these final actions had been marred by poor planning and tactics by the British. Lessons that may have been clear after Bir el Mazar and Maghara – such as the need for the full and proper reconnaissance and mapping of enemy positions – had not been learned, nor had the lesson that, while spreading thinly to pin the enemy down had its uses, the attackers must have overwhelming numbers and firepower in one area to overcome the defenders rapidly and avoid a protracted fight. Failure to address these two issues would lead to further disasters in the following few months at the First and Second Battles of Gaza.

However, in the meantime, the over-arching British objective – securing the Suez Canal from direct attack and establishing a forward defensive line on the eastern side of the Sinai Desert – had been accomplished. This would prove a rare offensive strategic land victory for the British Empire. On the Western Front, the strategic successes so far had been defensive ones, holding back the Germans, and elsewhere successes had either been of little strategic importance (such as elsewhere in Africa) or had, after initial success, run into catastrophe, as in Mesopotamia. Although Murray was already looking to begin his next offensive, towards Gaza and into Palestine, the Sinai Campaign was over.

Three Australians pose in front of one of the Ottoman redoubts at El Magruntein.

TAKING THE REDUIT, EL MAGRUNTEIN, 9 JANUARY 1917 (PP. 86–87)

In the final two actions of the campaign the mounted troops were used to both their best and worst effects. Large bodies of mounted troops were able to cover long distances quickly and take Ottoman garrisons by surprise. However, once engaged, the troops dismounted and conducted conventional attacks where their relatively light weight of fire in terms of both artillery and musketry left them struggling to succeed. Only with courage and perseverance, and after the decision to withdraw had been made, was victory achieved in both cases.

At El Magruntein, the Ottoman positions were, as usual, extremely well sited but lacking in barbed wire or any other reinforcement **(1)**. The Ottomans had to rely on weight of fire alone, but given the open and bare ground around the defences this was initially enough to hold back the dismounted cavalry. It took most of the day for the New Zealand Mounted Rifles to work by fire and manoeuvre close enough to charge into Point 265 and then the Reduit **(2)**, taking the centre of the Ottoman defences. With their defences pierced, the Ottomans began to surrender **(3)**.

The NZMR wore slouch hats similar to the Light Horse, but of a different design **(4)**. However, the relentless sun, heat, sweat and other punishment generally pushed them out of any intentional shape fairly quickly. The Ottomans wear their distinctive 'enveriye' cap, whose structure led to significant variations in shape **(5)**. The officer **(6)** wears a green collar and edging on his enveriye's cloth strips that denote his branch as the infantry.

AFTERMATH

As befitted the slow, logistics-dominated campaign fought by the EEF through 1916, the months following the action at El Magruntein saw little offensive action while the railway caught up, water sources were developed and supplies stockpiled to support an increasingly large force at El Arish. The Ottomans were also content to limit their operations to developing their defences at Gaza and Beersheba, and at Tel el Sharia about midway between the two where a major logistics hub was developed.

In January 1917, the War Office ordered Murray to despatch one of his divisions to France, and he selected the 42nd Division, even while protesting that he needed one more, not one fewer, infantry division to protect Egypt. Nevertheless, in early February, the division embarked, and at roughly the same time the railway and pipeline finally reached El Arish. With the 52nd (Lowland) and 53rd (Welsh) Divisions at that post, and the 54th (East Anglian) Division at Romani, Murray was given permission to raise a fourth infantry division from the depots in the Nile Delta by merging dismounted Yeomanry regiments and forming the 74th (Yeomanry) Division, although the new formation was both disgruntled at losing its horses and would be short of heavy equipment and support troops for some time. At the same time, other British and Australian mounted units in Egypt were brought forward to create enough brigades to form a new cavalry formation, the Imperial Mounted Division.

Murray was operating under orders from the War Office that required careful balancing: to maintain the pressure on the Ottomans, but not to become involved in major actions. With the British Imperial forces still recovering from the Somme offensive in France, and with growing commitments in Salonika and Mesopotamia, the War Office did not want to have to commit increased resources to Egypt. However, Murray continued to push his troops forward, re-occupying Shiekh Zowaiid and then Rafa, and he felt that an attack on Gaza could not only be successful but also give him a strong position from which to eventually invade Palestine. Gaza was in a strong position dominating the border between Egypt and Palestine, and every invading army to have turned that particular geographical corner, from the Pharaohs to Napoleon Bonaparte, had had to take Gaza first.

In his estimation of the coming attack, Murray was working on several erroneous conclusions that had developed during the Sinai Campaign. It was felt that the Ottomans would not stand if attacked vigorously (despite the still recent experience of Gallipoli). The rearguard actions after Romani, where the Ottomans had staged a well-ordered fighting retreat, had been

The move into the border regions brought the troops into a more fertile area, with more agriculture and natural foliage to help sustain the horses, easing the supply problems and improving the health of the mounts.

completely misunderstood. One reason for fully encircling the garrisons at Magdhaba and El Magruntein had been the idea that the Ottoman forces would simply slip away if allowed to do so. Equally, the lessons from those two actions relating to the need for effective reconnaissance, forward planning, adequate artillery and the general fighting ability of the Ottoman soldier were all ignored.

On 26 March 1917, General Dobell launched two infantry and two mounted divisions at Gaza. While the two mounted divisions cast a broad net around the city to capture the garrison as it tried to escape, the 53rd (Welsh) Division, supported by the 54th (East Anglian) Division, found themselves advancing through thick mist while the commanders of that division, the Desert Column, and the Eastern Force all waited for visibility to improve so that they could see the enemy positions and formulate their plans. The resulting attack was a fiasco created by poor communications, almost non-existent planning, lack of intelligence and a fundamental misjudgement of the capabilities of the enemy. What had so nearly happened at Magdhaba and El Magruntein happened on a much larger scale at Gaza, and the EEF was repulsed with 4,500 casualties.

Murray obfuscated the events and results of the battle in his despatch to the War Office, and despite the wishes of Prime Minister Lloyd George to replace him, they replied by ordering him to make a further attack in mid-April. News had arrived that Baghdad had fallen in Mesopotamia, and it was hoped that some kind of momentum could be built up in the war against the Ottomans. However, while the EEF was reinforced and even received small numbers of tanks and amounts of poison gas, the Second Battle of Gaza from 17 to 19 April was also a disaster. The tanks and gas were ill-used, and the increased attacking force was spread across a wide front both at Gaza and for some distance down the Gaza–Beersheba road. Meanwhile, the Ottomans had been busy developing their defences, creating deep trench systems around Gaza and a string of redoubts and systems along the road to Beersheba. As usual, these were well-sited and strong positions, and again the British were spread over a broad area without the necessary weight to break through in any one place. In those few places that British troops managed to enter Ottoman redoubts or systems, swift and effective Ottoman counter-attacks pushed them back. This time, the lesson on Ottoman military efficiency cost the EEF 6,500 casualties.

After the Second Battle of Gaza, the British at least maintained their forward positions and began to dig in, and complex trench systems began to be developed by both sides to the south and south-east of Gaza, petering out into outposts and cavalry piquets further east into the desert. Although the EEF continued to raid the Ottoman trenches and mount sometimes large and complicated cavalry raids on the desert flank, the battle effectively became a static one. The second failure gave Lloyd George the leverage he needed to finally get rid of Murray, and in late June, General Sir Edmund Allenby arrived to replace him. With Allenby came reinforcements in terms of troops, artillery, aircraft and other materiel, all of which, in fairness to him, Murray had been requesting all spring.

Both the EEF and the Ottomans would embark on long processes of reinforcement and reorganization through the summer and autumn, each readying to retake the offensive. The Ottomans planned to make a final, and much larger, attempt to recapture the Sinai and cut the Suez Canal with their Yildirim Battle Group, a force that would consist of 18 of the 45 infantry divisions that formed the entire Ottoman Army. General Allenby would manage to make his move first, attacking Beersheba on 31 October 1917, and capturing both Jaffa and Jerusalem by the end of the year. The blow, and the loss of stockpiled munitions and equipment, would be one from which the Ottoman Empire would never recover. It would also bring a complete and final end to any threats to the Suez Canal.

A funeral at Romani. The men buried in these graves were later reburied in the cemeteries in the Nile Delta. Those with no known grave from the campaign are remembered on the Memorial to the Missing in Jerusalem War Cemetery, on Mount Scopus.

THE BATTLEFIELD TODAY

Much of the northern Sinai Desert today is considered too dangerous to visit. A number of Islamic extremist groups are active in the area, and the British Foreign and Commonwealth Office, US State Department and Australian Department of Foreign Affairs and Trade all strongly recommend their citizens do not enter. Even if they were reachable by tourists, over a century of shifting sands will have left little if any trace of the 1916 battles.

However, some associated sites are still accessible. The Commonwealth War Graves Commission maintains numerous cemeteries in the Nile Delta, containing casualties from the Sinai Campaign as well as Gallipoli and World War II. The cemeteries at Alexandria (Hadra), Cairo War Memorial, Port Said War Memorial and Kantara all contain casualties from the Sinai. A memorial at Heliopolis commemorates the Indian contribution, and a

The restored Ottoman railway station at Be'er Sheva (Beersheba), now opened as a museum.

small memorial at Kantara records the New Zealand casualties from Romani and El Magruntein with no known grave.

In Giza, there is a remarkable memorial to the men of the Egyptian Labour Corps and the Camel Transport Corps in the form of an ophthalmic laboratory, in the grounds of an eye hospital. The building was still functioning as a laboratory at the time of writing, and on the outside walls, several bronze plaques commemorate the work of the ELC.

On the other side of the Sinai, equally few signs of the 1916 campaign remain. The names of those members of the EEF or other British forces who were killed in the Sinai but have no known graves are recorded on the Memorial to the Missing that forms the back wall of the Jerusalem War Cemetery on Mount Scopus. Several elements of the Ottoman railway network, so crucial to their logistics, survive in Jerusalem, where the pre-war First Station is now a boutique shopping centre; at Semakh at the southern tip of the Sea of Galilee; and at Be'er Sheva, where a small museum now occupies the station buildings. About 35km (20 miles) west of Be'er Sheva, a small, and slightly later, fragment of the British railway system can be found at Eshkol National Park, where there is a short piece of narrow-gauge track, a bridge fragment and a replica carriage.

In the UK, there is only a single memorial that is dedicated to a unit that served only in the EEF. A memorial in the Victoria Embankment Gardens on the Thames Embankment in London is dedicated to the men of the Imperial Camel Corps.

A replica British railway carriage near a restored section of rail and bridge at Eshkol National Park, Israel.

BIBLIOGRAPHY

Anglesey, Marquis of, *A History of the British Cavalry 1816–1919, Vol. 5: Egypt, Palestine and Syria 1914 to 1919*, Leo Cooper: London (1994)
Anon., *The Fifth Battalion Highland Light Infantry in the War, 1914–1918*, MacLehose, Jackson & Co.: Glasgow (1921)
Benn, Captain William Wedgwood DSO DFC, *In the Side Shows*, P. S. Chapman: Auckland (2010)
Bluett, Anthony, *A Gunner's Crusade*, Leonaur Ltd: London (2007)
Bourne, Lieutenant Colonel G. H., *History of the 2nd Light Horse Regiment AIF*, Northern Daily Leader: Tamworth (1926)
Cutlack, F. M., *Official History of Australia in the War of 1914–18, Vol. 8: The Australian Flying Corps*, Angus and Robertson Ltd: Sydney (1923)
Djemal Pasha, *Memories of a Turkish Statesman, 1913–19*, Hutchinson & Co.: London (1922)
Erickson, Lieutenant Colonel Edward, *Ordered to Die: A History of the Ottoman Army in the First World War*, Greenwood Press: London (2001)
Erickson, Lieutenant Colonel Edward, *Ottoman Army Effectiveness in World War I: A Comparative Study*, Routledge: Abingdon (2007)
Gullett, H. S., *Official History of Australia in the War of 1914–18, Vol. 7: The AIF in Sinai and Palestine, 1914–18*, Angus and Robertson Ltd: Sydney (1923)
Hadaway, Stuart, *Pyramids and Fleshpots: The Egyptian, Senussi and Eastern Mediterranean Campaigns, 1914–16*, Spellmount: London (2014)
Hamilton OBE, Patrick M., *Riders of Destiny: The 4th Australian Light Horse Field Ambulance 1917–18*, Mostly Unsung Military History: Gardenvale (1995)
Hatton, S. F., *The Yarn of a Yeoman*, Naval & Military Press Ltd: Uckfield (1930)
Hill, Group Captain C. W., *The Spook and the Commandant*, William Kimber & Co. Ltd: London (1975)
Inchbald, Geoffrey, *With the Imperial Camel Corps in the Great War*, Leonaur Ltd: London (2005)
Jones, Captain H. A., *The War in the Air, Vol. 5*, Oxford University Press: Oxford (1935)
Kressenstein, Friedrich Freiherr Kress von, *Bayerischer General Und Orientkenner. Lebenserinnerungen, Tagebücher Und Berichte 1914–1946*, Brill Schoningh: Paderborn (2020)
MacMunn KCB KCSI DSO, Lieutenant General Sir G., and Captain C. Falls, *Military Operations: Egypt and Palestine Vol. 1*, HMSO: London (1928)
Moore, Lieutenant A. B., *The Mounted Rifleman in Sinai and Palestine*, Whitcombe & Tombs Ltd: Auckland (1920)
Murray, General Sir Archibald, *Sir Archibald Murray's Despatches*, HMSO: London (1920)
Powles, Colonel C. G. (ed.), *The History of the Canterbury Mounted Rifles, 1914–19*, Whitcombe & Tombs Ltd: Auckland (1928)
Sanders, General Liman von, *Five Years in Turkey*, US Naval Institute: Annapolis (1928)
Thompson, Lieutenant Colonel R. R., *The Fifty-Second Lowland Division 1914–1918*, Maclehose, Jackson & Co.: Glasgow (1923)
Uyar, Mesut, *The Ottoman Army and the First World War*, Routledge: Abingdon (2021)
Woodward, David, *Forgotten Soldiers of the First World War*, Tempus Publishing Ltd: Stroud (2007)

INDEX

Figures in **bold** refer to illustrations.

Allenby, General Sir Edmund 91

Beersheba 40, 64, **92**, 93
Bir Bayud **62**, 72–73
Bir el Abd 38, **62**, 64, **68–69**
Bir el Mazar, attack on 32, 47, **62**, 67–75, **68–69**
Bir el Tawal 74
Bir Salama 50
Bluett, Gunner Anthony 49
Bourne, Lieutenant Colonel G. 55
British and Imperial Forces 21–26
    aircraft 25, 35, **36**, 70, 71, **72**, 74
    Royal Navy:
        Anne, HMS 25
        Ben-My-Chree, HMS 25, 71
        Empress, HMS 25
        Espiegle, HMS 25, 71
        M15, HMS 71
        M31, HMS 71
        Raven II, HMS 25
    East Indies and Egypt Seaplane Squadron **75**
    Egyptian Expeditionary Force (EEF) 7, 64
    corps sized:
        Desert Mounted Corps 16
        Eastern Force 73
        No. 1 Canal Section 73
        No. 2 Canal Section 52, 73
        No. 3 Canal Section 51, 73
        Northern Canal Section 73
        Southern Canal Section 73
    corps formations:
        Army Ordnance Corps 39
        Army Service Corps 39
        Army Veterinary Corps 39
        Australian Flying Corps 50, 77, 82, 84
        Bikaner Camel Corps 39, **47**
        Camel Transport Corps 25, 48, **66**, 93
        Egyptian Labour Corps 25, 48, **66**, 93
        Royal Artillery 23, **25**
        Royal Engineers 37, 39
        Royal Flying Corps **36**, 47, 50, 77, 82, 84
    divisions:
        42nd (East Lancashire) Division 30, 31, 37, 52, 61, 76, 89
        52nd (Lowland) Division 14, 31, 37, 51, 55, 61, 76, 89
        53rd (Welsh) Division 37, 51, 89
        54th (East Anglian) Division 37, 89
        74th (Yeomanry) Division 89

        Australian and New Zealand Mounted Division 7, 15, 31, 51, 52, 54, 61, 64, 71
        Imperial Mounted Division 89
    brigades:
        1st Australian Light Horse Brigade 15, 51, 54, 63–64, 70, 77, 80–82
        2nd Australian Light Horse Brigade 51, 54, 55, 60, 63–64, 70
        3rd Australian Light Horse Brigade 51, 61, 63, 70, 77, 80–85
        5th Mounted Brigade 37–39, 51, 55, 61, 63, 85
        125th Brigade 63
        127th Brigade 63
        155th Brigade 59
        156th Brigade 59, 61
        158th Brigade 51
        Imperial Camel Corps Brigade 24, 31, 37, 70, **73**, 74, 76–77, 80–81, 93
        Imperial Service Cavalry Brigade 23
        New Zealand Mounted Rifles Brigade 7, 24, 51, **52**, 59, 61, 77, 80–82
    regiments and battalions:
        1st City of London Yeomanry 72
        1st Australian Light Horse Regiment 54
        2nd Australian Light Horse Regiment 54–55
        3rd Australian Light Horse Regiment 55
        5th Australian Light Horse Regiment 39, 51, 66
        6th Australian Light Horse Regiment 55
        7th Australian Light Horse Regiment 55
        8th Australian Light Horse Regiment 85
        10th Australian Light Horse Regiment 80, 81
        11th Australian Light Horse Regiment 72
        12th Australian Light Horse Regiment 72
        Auckland Mounted Rifles 81
        Canterbury Mounted Rifles 84
        Highland Light Infantry **48**
        Manchester Regiment **22**
        Norfolk Yeomanry 7, **30**
        Queen's Own Royal Glasgow Yeomanry 39

        Queen's Own Worcestershire Hussars (Yeomanry) 37, 37–39, **38**, 41, 47, 59
        Royal Gloucestershire Hussars (Yeomanry) 37, 39, 41, 47, 59
        Royal Scots Fusiliers 39
        Scottish Rifles 61, 63
        Suffolk Yeomanry 7
        Warwickshire Yeomanry 37–39
        Wellington Mounted Rifles 51, 55, **64**
    squadrons:
        No. 1 Squadron AFC 25
        No. 14 Squadron RFC 24–25, 70
        No. 17 Squadron RFC 25
        No. 413 Squadron RE 37
        Port Said Seaplane Squadron 25, **75**
    batteries:
        7th Light Car Patrol 82, 84, 85
        Ayrshire Battery RHA 59
        B Battery HAC 82
        Hong Kong and Singapore Mountain Battery 70, 72, 82
        Inverness Battery RHA 77, 82, 84
        Leicester Battery RHA 82
        Somerset Battery RHA 77, 82

Canterbury Hill 51, **53**
casualty clearing stations **36**
Chauvel, Major-General Sir Henry **15**, 15–16, 31, 51, 59, 80–81
Chaytor, Major-General Edward 80
Chetwode, Lieutenant-General Sir Philip 73, 82
concert parties **71**
conscription 21, 25
Coventry, Lieutenant Colonel the Hon. Charles 39, 41, 46, 47
Cox, Brigadier-General Charles 81
Cripps, Lieutenant E. T. 59

Dallas, Major-General Alister 72
Damascus 34
Dawnay, Brigadier-General Sir Guy 18
Djemal, Ahmed Pasha 6, **10**, 10–11, 65
Dobell, Lieutenant-General Sir Charles 73, 90
Dueidar 37, 39

El Arish 32, **32**, 35, 50, 54, 65, 67, **68–69**
    Wadi 76, 78–79, 80
El Magruntein 31, 77, 82–85, **83**, **85**, **86–87**, 88 *see also* Rafa

Falkenhayn, Field Marshal von 12

Gaza 16, 64, 89–91
German and Austrian Forces
    aircraft 20, **20**, 23, 71
    Flieger Abteilung (FA) 300: 20, **20**, 35, 71
    machine-gun companies 20–21, **59**
    Pasha Force 20–21
Giza 93

Hafr al Auja 76
Hafr Enna 63
Hamisah 37, 38–39, 41
Hedjaz Railway 34
Hill 70: 39, 52
Hod el Enna 63

Ibrahim, Colonel 54
Inchbald, Geoffrey 74

Jaffa 34, 64, 91
Jerusalem 34, 65, 91, 93
Jifjafa 35, 50

kabalak hat 18
Kantara 34, 37, 65, 93
Katib Gannit 50, 52, **53** 55, 59
Khadir Bey, Colonel 80, **80**, 81
Khamsin wind 50
Kressenstein, General Frederich Freiherr Kress von 6–7, 11–12, **12**, 19, 34, 54, 64

Lawrence, Major-General the Hon. Sir Herbert **14**, 14–15, 31, 51, 52
Lloyd-Baker, Captain Michael 40, 47
Lloyd George, David 90–91
locusts, plagues of 11, 34

Magdhaba 31, 77, 78–79
Mageibra 38, 39

Maghara **62**, 71
Maxwell, General Sir John 31
memorials 92–93
Meredith, Lieutenant Colonel John 54
Meyer, Major 54
Mitla Pass 74
Moiya Harab 50
Moore, Lieutenant A. Briscoe 24
Mount Meredith 53, 55
Mount Royston 51, 52, **53**, 55, 60
Muhlman, Major 54
Murray, General Sir Archibald 7, **13**, 13–14, 33, 65, 89, 91

Nekhl 74

Oghratina 38, 39–40, **42–43**, **62**, 64
orders of battle 26–27
Ottoman Army 17–21
    1st Expeditionary Corps 34
    1st Expeditionary Force 54
    4th Army 6
    3rd Cavalry Division 65
    3rd Infantry Division:
        31st Regiment 54, 67, 82
        32nd Regiment 36, 54
        39th Regiment 54, 67
        80th Regiment 80, **80**
    Hedjaz Camel Regiment 21, 36
    Yildirim Battle Group 91

Pelusium Station 51, 52, **53**, 61
pipelines 48–49, 89
Port Said 25, 35, 92
prisoners **60**, **61**
pumps, water 66

Qatia, affair at 15, 29, **29**, 31, 37–47, **38**, **39**, **41**, **42–43**, **44–45**, 46

Rafa 15, 31, **84**, 89 *see also* El Magruntein
railways 34, 48, 66, 77, 89, **93**
rations 49–50, 60–61
Refet, Colonel 54
Roberts, Captain Frederick 39
Romani, Battle of 15, 16, 48–66, **51**, **53**, 55, **55**, **56–57**, 58, **91**
Royston, Brigadier-General Sir John 'Galloping Jack' 54, 60

Salmana **62**, 67, **68–69**
Sanders, General Liman von 11, 19
Shiekh Zowaiid 82, 89
sickness 49–50
Sinai Desert **4**, **29**, 67
Smith, General Wilfred 31, 51, 59
Suez Canal 5–6, **6**

Taba Crisis 5
Tel el Sharia 30, 64, 89
trenches **17**, 37

uniforms 18, 21–22, **23**

Wadi um Mukhsheid 50
water supply 11, 48–49, 61, 66, 75–76
weapons 18, 22, **25**, 50, 51, **52**
Wellington Ridge 50–51, 52, **53**, 55, 59, 60, 61
Wiggin, Brigadier-General Edgar 37–38, 41
Wiggin, Captain William 'Bill' 46
Williams-Thomas, Major Frank 38, 40
Wilson, Lieutenant Colonel Lachlan 66

Yorke, Lieutenant Colonel Ralph 41, 47